IN DEFENSE OF WOMEN

H. L. MENCKEN

IN DEFENSE OF

WOMEN

TIME Reading Program Special Edition

Time-Life Books Inc., Alexandria, Virginia

Time-Life Books Inc.
is a wholly owned subsidiary of
TIME INCORPORATED

TIME Reading Program: *Editor*, Max Gissen

Library of Congress CIP data following page 172.

For information about any Time-Life book, please write:
Reader Information, Time-Life Books,
541 North Fairbanks Court, Chicago, Illinois 60611

CONTENTS

EDITORS' PREFACE

Show an educated American between the ages of 50 and 80 the words "an equestrian statue of Susan B. Anthony, the apostle of woman suffrage" and the chances are good that he will recognize them as produced by the riotous imagination of Henry Louis Mencken. Americans under 45 are much less likely to identify the signature of the Sage of Baltimore who, after 20 years of extraordinary influence upon the mental climate of his time, suddenly went out of fashion in the 1930s, a victim of his own success. He could not stand up against a new idiomatic tide that glorified the common man, even though that tide sprang in part from depths containing a thoroughly Menckenian contempt for the common man.

The mass defection of most of the Mencken cult
into the arms of the New Deal was one of the most
significant ironies of 20th Century American life. It
left hanging questions as to what Mencken had really
been up to, whether he had been a buffoon or a philosopher, where he fitted into the intellectual, social and
political history of his critical time. Those who in their
youth read Mencken with surprised delight will find
a new kind of interest in reading him now amid the
debris of burnt-out battles. Those who were too young
to read him then will, by reading him now, acquire an
indispensable key to the American day-before-yester-
day, which is, of course, the key to tomorrow. Besides,
there are extra dividends. Not only was Mencken the
medium through which certain peculiar attitudes entered the American psyche; he was also the ringmaster
of one of the most astounding verbal circuses ever
put on the road. He was a stylist with a heavy touch,
but his smoking typewriter reminted every thought
that passed through it. The philosophy was sometimes
dubious but the outrageous fun was genuine, and time
has not dimmed it.

On all counts, from the serious to the frivolous, his
In Defense of Women offers an effective retrospect on
Mencken. In it the Mencken of 1918 caught "the woman
question" at the beginning of one of those waves of
change which for 2,000 years have intermittently
troubled the Western world. He noted, long before the
vacuum cleaner's hysterical whine was universally
heard in the land, that the increased leisure of American women had created problems for them—a theme

which sociologists, divorce court judges and psychiatrists are still spinning. "Thousands of [women] have been emancipated from any compulsion to productive labor without having acquired any compensatory intellectual or artistic interest or social duty," he commented. "The result is that they swarm in the women's clubs and waste their time listening to bad poetry, worse music and still worse lectures on Maeterlinck, Balkan politics and the subconscious."

It is quickly apparent that *In Defense of Women* is *not* a defense of women. Woman's self-appointed advocate soon exposes his client unmercifully. "The average woman, until art comes to her aid, is ungraceful, misshapen, badly calved and crudely articulated, even for a woman. If she has a good torso, she is almost sure to be bowlegged. If she has good legs, she is almost sure to have bad teeth. If she has good teeth, she is almost sure to have scrawny hands, or muddy eyes, or hair like oakum, or no chin." She cannot cook or keep house. Her reputation for piety is bogus. "I have said that the religion preached by Jesus, now totally extinct in this world, was highly favorable to women. This was not saying, of course, that women have repaid the compliment by adopting it." As for ethics, "women not only bite in the clinches; they bite even in open fighting; they have a dental reach, so to speak, of amazing length."

The book, indeed, so abounds with insults to the unfair sex that when it was first published many women, whether conventional or emancipated, hurled it across the room. But it is not correct to conclude that the title is meant sarcastically and that the book is in reality an attack on women. On the contrary, it is an attack on men. The implicit syllogism of the work is: Women are despicable; but women are better than men; therefore, men are very despicable. "I am convinced," says Mencken in the book, "that the average woman, whatever her deficiencies, is greatly superior to the average man."

And that brings us to the *why* of this book, a matter that can be probed only by understanding the relation between three entities, all named H. L. Mencken. Mencken the Man was sociable, outgoing, alert, infinitely kind, fond of all that is good in life, including women. Mencken the Artist had also an outgoing, even a gregarious quality, for his first success was as a newspaperman—that is, as one who addresses the popular mass. The third Mencken, the Devotee, jarred against these other two, for the object of his devotion was the revolutionary philosophy of Friedrich Nietzsche, who despised the Judaeo-Christian "slave morality," hated democracy and "the herd," and cried for the emergence of Supermen. (There was also a fourth Mencken not pertinent to this discussion—the self-taught philologist whose sensitive ear and patient, roughhewn scholarship produced *The American Language*.)

In his introduction to an edition of *In Defense of Women* published in 1922, Mencken, explaining how he came to write the book, gives a clue to its real motivation. He recalls with indignation that a volume of his essays during the 1914-1918 World War had run into censorship trouble, that there was a general air of intolerance to new ideas and that he had therefore resolved to write on a subject far removed from international politics and moreover "to make this brochure upon the woman question extremely *pianissimo* in tone, and to avoid burdening it with any ideas of an unfamiliar, and hence illegal nature." This is a small part of the truth. Mencken's wartime difficulties were real, his pro-German (or rather his antidemocratic) feelings being well known. Yet resistance to Nietzschean doctrine was as strong in peacetime as it had been in war; if Mencken the Devotee was to function, Mencken the Artist had to find a form that would smuggle the doctrine past a censorship, not of officials, but of the reader's own faith in his society's principles and practices. *In Defense of Women* was such a smuggling operation.

For example, the Nietzschean aphorism "[Woman] should be educated . . . for the recreation of the warrior" seemed disgusting to Americans of that day—as it does to Americans of this. But the same attitude can be expressed indirectly. Here is what Mencken the popular Artist did with it:

"Every man, I daresay, has his own notion of what constitutes perfect peace and contentment, but all of those notions, despite the fundamental conflict of the sexes, revolve around women. As for me—I reject the two commonest of them: passion, at least in its more adventurous and melodramatic aspects, is too exciting and alarming for so indolent a man, and I am too egoistic to have much desire to be mothered. What, then, remains for me? Let me try to describe it to you.

"It is the close of a busy and vexatious day—say half past five or six o'clock of a winter afternoon. I have had a cocktail or two, and am stretched out on a divan in front of a fire, smoking. At the edge of the divan, close enough for me to reach her with my hand, sits a woman not too young, but still good-looking and well-dressed—above all a woman with a soft, low-pitched, agreeable voice. As I snooze she talks—of anything, everything, all the things that women talk of: books, music, the play, men, other women. No politics. No business. No religion. No metaphysics. Nothing challenging and vexatious—but remember, she is intelligent; what she says is clearly expressed, and often picturesquely. I observe the fine sheen of her hair, the pretty cut of her frock, the glint of her white teeth, the arch of her eyebrow, the graceful curve of her arm. I listen to the exquisite murmur of her voice. Gradually I fall asleep—but only for an instant. At once, observing it, she raises her voice ever so little, and I am awake. Then to sleep again—slowly and charmingly down that slippery hill of dreams. And then awake again, and then asleep again, and so on. I ask you seriously: could anything be more unutterably beautiful?"

Thus indeed spake Zarathustra or some other Oriental voice. It is no wonder that umbrage was taken, as Mencken later told one of his biographers, by the woman who identified herself as the heroine of this revolting vignette in which she appears as an improved version of a cuckoo clock.

In a broader and more serious vein Mencken's influence struck deep. His minor premise in this book is that women are better than men. Better in what way? Because women are "less civilized." Because women disdain all the practical skills of the world—law because it is a sham, politics because it is unspeakably low, busiess because it is a degrading and childish occupation.

Again and again Mencken drove home this disdain for the elements of American civilization, not only in his books but in his editing of *The Smart Set* and *The American Mercury*. His influence was immense in the late '20s, especially among the nation's college students. It helped to turn intellectuals against the business community and toward a highly emotional form of politics that substituted for the direct decisions of "average men" the control of central government, which they deemed to be superior in wisdom.

Mencken, of course, hated the results. A violent anti-New Dealer, he never understood that he had had an inadvertent hand in setting up the leftward swing of American intellectuals. The '30s were bitter years for him, although they began brightly with his marriage in 1930, when he was 50, to Sara Haardt, a teacher at Goucher College who was 22 years younger. She was in many respects an unlikely mate for Mencken; in selecting her he was forced to beat simultaneous retreats on several fronts. He had railed for years against the South; she came from Montgomery, Alabama. Although he approved of the vote for women on the ground that women would have sense enough to abolish democracy, he despised active suffragettes; Sara when very young had led suffrage rallies. He had made disparaging remarks about "lady novelists"; but he encouraged her in writing a novel, *The Making of a Lady*. Worst of all, she drank Alabama's *vin du pays,* Coca-Cola; Mencken on one occasion thoughtfully saw to it that their cabin on a North German Lloyd liner was well stocked with bottles of the pause that refreshes, though he himself was a dedicated beer-bibber.

The marriage was clouded only by Mrs. Mencken's ill-health and by the persistent, ghoulish glee with which the press dug up Mencken's previous harsh words about marriage, especially from *In Defense of Women*. The most superior men, he had said, were not ever trapped into matrimony. And though he had granted that some superior men, late in life, married much younger women, he had offered an explanation that haunted him now: "It is not that age calls maudlinly to youth, as the poets would have it; it is that age is no match for youth, especially when age is male and youth is female." Quotations of this sort became embarrassing to Mencken. He could not quite laugh them off; he took his myth seriously, as a popular artist must. He forbade further reissues of *In Defense of Women* and except for the publication of this special edition it has been out of print since 1932.

Sara Mencken died in 1935. After that, Mencken again underwent the strain of living through a war in which his heart was not wholly on the side of the democracies. Before the end, however, the Man and the Artist almost buried the Nietzschean Devotee in three charming autobiographical books, *Happy Days, News-*

paper Days and *Heathen Days*. His style ran clear and much more quietly. The ranting vanished. Whatever had been worth-while in all his previous diatribes against "conventional morality" and "romantic bilge" was better said in a little story contained in *Newspaper Days* and called "A Girl from Red Lion, P.A."

"A rosy-cheeked young woman, carrying a pasteboard suitcase and a pink parasol" alighted from a train in Baltimore and asked a hack driver to convey her to "a house of ill-fame." The driver, Peebles, an honest man sensing that he was in the presence of innocence, took his fare to the house of ill-fame with the best reputation he knew, that of Miss Nellie d'Alembert who, according to Mencken, "though she lacked the polish of Vassar, had sound sense, a pawky humor and progressive ideas." As soon as Miss Nellie heard the girl's remarkable story, a case of life imitating art, she sent for Mencken, then a young journalist, and he in turn brought into consultation a colleague named Percy Heath.

The girl, it seemed, had been seduced as recently as the night before last by her friend Elmer, with whom she shared an interest in the romantic books of that time (circa 1905) wherein the heroine, once she had erred, invariably left home, embarked on a life of shame, "took to booze and dope and died in the gutter." Reflecting on these books, she lay awake all night after she had kicked Elmer out, "rose much troubled next morning" and, resolving to bow to the horrible fate she considered inevitable, sneaked away from home and took the night train to Baltimore.

Mencken, Percy Heath and Miss Nellie d'Alembert persuaded the girl that the books were out of date and that she did not need to act out the whole grim story that their moralism foretold. Her eyes brimming with tears of gratitude, and none the worse for her journey to Baltimore, she returned to her bucolic home near Red Lion, P.A.

So you see, Mencken the Man was quite capable of acting chivalrously in defense of women—a quality the reader will not necessarily discern from *In Defense of Women,* a polemical book by Mencken the Artist pursuing the purposes of Mencken the Nietzschean Devotee.

—THE EDITORS

AUTHOR'S INTRODUCTION

As a professional critic of life and letters, my principal business in the world is that of manufacturing platitudes for tomorrow, which is to say, ideas so novel that they will be instantly rejected as insane and outrageous by all right-thinking men, and so apposite and sound that they will eventually conquer that instinctive opposition, and force themselves into the traditional wisdom of the race. I hope I need not confess that a large part of my stock in trade consists of platitudes rescued from the cobwebbed shelves of yesterday, with new labels stuck rakishly upon them. This borrowing and refurbishing of shop-worn goods, as a matter of fact, is the invariable habit of traders in ideas, at all times and everywhere. It is not, however, that all the

conceivable human notions have been thought out; it
is simply, to be quite honest, that the sort of men
who volunteer to think out new ones seldom, if ever,
have wind enough for a full day's work. The most
they can ever accomplish in the way of genuine originality is an occasional brilliant spurt, and half a
dozen such spurts, particularly if they come close together and show a certain co-ordination, are enough
to make a practitioner celebrated, and even immortal.
Nature, indeed, conspires against all such genuine
originality, and I have no doubt that God is against
it on His heavenly throne, as His vicars and partisans
unquestionably are on this earth. The dead hand
pushes all of us into intellectual cages; there is in all
of us a strange tendency to yield and have done. Thus
the impertinent colleague of Aristotle is doubly beset,
first by a public opinion that regards his enterprise as
subversive and in bad taste, and secondly by an inner
weakness that limits his capacity for it, and especially
his capacity to throw off the prejudices and superstitions of his race, culture and time. The cell, said
Haeckel, does not act, it *re*acts—and what is the instru-
ment of reflection and speculation save a congeries of
cells? At the moment of the contemporary meta-
physician's loftiest flight, when he is most gratefully
warmed by the feeling that he is far above all the
ordinary air lanes and has an absolutely novel concept
by the tail, he is suddenly pulled up by the discovery
that what is entertaining him is simply the ghost of
some ancient idea that his school-master forced into
him in 1887, or the mouldering corpse of a doctrine

that was made official in his country during the late war, or a sort of fermentation-product, to mix the figure, of a banal heresy launched upon him recently by his wife. This is the penalty that the man of intellectual curiosity and vanity pays for his violation of the divine edict that what has been revealed from Sinai shall suffice for him, and for his resistance to the natural process which seeks to reduce him to the respectable level of a patriot and taxpayer.

I was, of course, privy to this difficulty when I planned the present work, and entered upon it with no expectation that I should be able to embellish it with, at most, more than a very small number of hitherto unutilized notions. Moreover, I faced the additional handicap of having an audience of extraordinary antipathy to ideas before me, for I wrote it in war-time, with all foreign markets cut off, and so my only possible customers were Americans. Of their unprecedented dislike for novelty in the domain of the intellect I have often discoursed in the past, and so there is no need to go into the matter again. All I need do here is to recall the fact that, in the United States, alone among the great nations of history, there is a right way to think and a wrong way to think in everything—not only in theology, or politics, or economics, but in the most trivial matters of everyday life. Thus, in the average American city the citizen who, in the face of an organized public clamour (usually managed by interested parties) for the erection of an equestrian statue of Susan B. Anthony, the apostle of woman suffrage, in front of the chief railway station, or the

purchase of a dozen leopards for the municipal zoo,
or the dispatch of an invitation to the Structural Iron
Workers' Union to hold its next annual convention in
the town Symphony Hall—the citizen who, for any
logical reason, opposes such a proposal—on the ground,
say, that Miss Anthony never mounted a horse in her
life, or that a dozen leopards would be less useful than
a gallows to hang the City Council, or that the Structural Iron Workers would spit all over the floor of
Symphony Hall and knock down the busts of Bach,
Beethoven and Brahms—this citizen is commonly de-
nounced as an anarchist and a public enemy. It is not
only erroneous to think thus; it has come to be immoral. And so on many other planes, high and low.
For an American to question any of the articles of
fundamental faith cherished by the majority is for
him to run grave risks of social disaster. The old
English offence of "imagining the King's death" has
been formally revived by the American courts, and
hundreds of men and women are in jail for com-
mitting it, and it has been so enormously extended
that, in some parts of the country at least, it now
embraces such remote acts as believing that the negroes
should have equality before the law, and speaking the
language of countries recently at war with the Republic, and conveying to a private friend a formula
for making synthetic gin. All such toyings with illicit
ideas are construed as *attentats* against democracy,
which, in a sense, perhaps they are. For democracy
is grounded upon so childish a complex of fallacies
that they must be protected by a rigid system of taboos,

else even half-wits would argue it to pieces. Its first concern must thus be to penalize the free play of ideas. In the United States this is not only its first concern, but also its last concern. No other enterprise, not even the trade in public offices and contracts, occupies the rulers of the land so steadily, or makes heavier demands upon their ingenuity and their patriotic passion.

Familiar with the risks flowing out of it—and having just had to change the plates of my "Book of Prefaces," a book of purely literary criticism, wholly without political purpose or significance, in order to get it through the mails, I determined to make this brochure upon the woman question extremely *pianissimo* in tone, and to avoid burdening it with any ideas of an unfamiliar, and hence illegal nature. So deciding, I presently added a *bravura* touch: the unquenchable vanity of the intellectual snob asserting itself over all prudence. That is to say, I laid down the rule that no idea should go into the book that was not already so obvious that it had been embodied in the proverbial philosophy, or folk-wisdom, of some civilized nation, including the Chinese. To this rule I remained faithful throughout. In its original form, as published in 1918, the book was actually just such a *pastiche* of proverbs, many of them English, and hence familiar even to Congressmen, newspaper editors and other such illiterates. It was not always easy to hold to this program; over and over again I was tempted to insert notions that seemed to have escaped the peasants of Europe and Asia. But in the end, at some cost to the form of the work, I managed to get through it without compromise, and so it was put into type. There is no need to add that my ideational abstinence went un-recognized and unrewarded. In fact, not a single American reviewer noticed it, and most of them slated the book violently as a mass of heresies and contumacies, a deliberate attack upon all the known and revered truths about the woman question, a headlong assault upon the national decencies. In the South, where the suspicion of ideas goes to extraordinary lengths, even for the United States, some of the newspapers actually denounced the book as German propaganda, designed to break down American *morale,* and called upon the Department of Justice to proceed against me for the crime known to American law as "criminal anarchy," *i.e.,* "imagining the King's death." Why the Comstocks did not forbid it the mails as lewd and lascivious I have never been able to determine. Certainly, they re-ceived many complaints about it. I myself, in fact, caused a number of these complaints to be lodged, in the hope that the resultant buffooneries would give me entertainment in those dull days of war, with all intellectual activities adjourned, and maybe promote the sale of the book. But the Comstocks were pursuing larger fish, and so left me to the righteous indignation of right-thinking reviewers, especially the suffragists. Their concern, after all, is not with books that are de-nounced; what they concentrate their moral passion on is the book that is praised.

The present edition is addressed to a wider audi-ence, in more civilized countries, and so I have felt free to introduce a number of propositions, not to be found in popular proverbs, that had to be omitted from the original edition. But even so, the book by no means pretends to preach revolutionary doctrines, or even doctrines of any novelty. All I design by it is to set down in more or less plain form certain ideas that practically every civilized man and woman holds *in petto,* but that have been concealed hitherto by the vast mass of sentimentalities swathing the whole woman question. It is a question of capital importance to all human beings, and it deserves to be discussed honestly and frankly, but there is so much of social reticence, of religious superstition and of mere emotion intermingled with it that most of the enormous literature it has thrown off is hollow and useless. I point for example, to the literature of the subsidiary question of woman suffrage. It fills whole libraries, but nine-tenths of it is merely rubbish, for it starts off from assumptions that are obviously untrue and it reaches conclusions that are at war with both logic and the facts. So with the question of sex specifically. I have read, literally, hundreds of volumes upon it, and uncountable numbers of pamphlets, handbills and inflammatory wall-cards, and yet it leaves the primary problem unsolved, which is to say, the problem as to what is to be done about the conflict between the celibacy enforced upon millions by civilization and the appetites implanted in all by God. In the main, it counsels yielding to celibacy, which is exactly as sensible as advising a dog to forget its fleas. Here, as in other fields, I do not presume to offer a remedy of my own. In truth, I am very suspicious of all remedies for the major ills of life, and believe that most of them are incurable. But I at least venture to discuss the matter realistically, and if what I have to say is not sagacious, it is at all events not evasive. This, I hope, is something. Maybe some later investigator will bring a better illumination to the subject.

—H. L. MENCKEN

IN DEFENSE OF WOMEN

I
THE
FEMININE
MIND

1. The Maternal Instinct

A MAN'S WOMEN folk, whatever their outward show of respect for his merit and authority, always regard him secretly as an ass, and with something akin to pity. His most gaudy sayings and doings seldom deceive them; they see the actual man within, and know him for a shallow and pathetic fellow. In this fact, perhaps, lies one of the best proofs of feminine intelligence, or, as the common phrase makes it, feminine intuition. The mark of that so-called intuition is simply a sharp and accurate perception of reality, an habitual immunity to emotional enchantment, a relentless capacity for distinguishing clearly between the appearance and the substance. The appearance, in the normal family

circle, is a hero, a magnifico, a demigod. The substance is a poor mountebank.

The proverb that no man is a hero to his valet is
obviously of masculine manufacture. It is both insincere and untrue: insincere because it merely masks
the egotistic doctrine that he is potentially a hero to
every one else, and untrue because a valet, being a
fourth-rate man himself, is likely to be the last person
in the world to penetrate his master's charlatanry. Who
ever heard of a valet who didn't envy his master
wholeheartedly? who wouldn't willingly change
places with his master? who didn't secretly wish that
he *was* his master? A man's wife labours under no
such naïve folly. She may envy her husband, true
enough, certain of his more soothing prerogatives and
sentimentalities. She may envy him his masculine
liberty of movement and occupation, his impenetrable
complacancy, his peasant-like delight in petty vices,
his capacity for hiding the harsh face of reality behind
the cloak of romanticism, his general innocence and
childishness. But she never envies him his puerile ego;
she never envies him his shoddy and preposterous
soul.

This shrewd perception of masculine bombast and
make-believe, this acute understanding of man as
the eternal tragic comedian, is at the bottom of that
compassionate irony which passes under the name of
the maternal instinct. A woman wishes to mother a
man simply because she sees into his helplessness, his
need of an amiable environment, his touching self-
delusion. That ironical note is not only daily apparent

in real life; it sets the whole tone of feminine fiction. The woman novelist, if she be skilful enough to arise out of mere imitation into genuine self-expression, never takes her heroes quite seriously. From the day of George Sand to the day of Selma Lagerlöf she has always got into her character study a touch of superior aloofness, of ill-concealed derision. I can't recall a single masculine figure created by a woman who is not, at bottom, a booby.

2. Women's Intelligence

HAT IT SHOULD still be necessary, at this late stage in the senility of the human race to argue that women have a fine and fluent intelligence is surely an eloquent proof of the defective observation, incurable prejudice, and general imbecility of their lords and masters. One finds very few professors of the subject, even among admitted feminists, approaching the fact as obvious; practically all of them think it necessary to bring up a vast mass of evidence to establish what should be an axiom. Even the Franco-Englishman, W. L. George, one of the most sharp-witted of the faculty, wastes a whole book upon the demonstration, and then, with a great air of uttering something new, gives it the humourless title of "The Intelligence of Women." The intelligence of women, forsooth! As well devote a laborious time to the sagacity of serpents, pickpockets, or Holy Church!

Women, in truth, are not only intelligent; they have almost a monopoly of certain of the subtler and more utile forms of intelligence. The thing itself, indeed, might be reasonably described as a special feminine character; there is in it, in more than one of its manifestations, a femaleness as palpable as the femaleness of cruelty, masochism or rouge. Men are strong. Men are brave in physical combat. Men have sentiment. Men are romantic, and love what they conceive to be virtue and beauty. Men incline to faith, hope and charity. Men know how to sweat and endure. Men are amiable and fond. But in so far as they show the true fundamentals of intelligence—in so far as they reveal a capacity for discovering the kernel of eternal verity in the husk of delusion and hallucination and a passion for bringing it forth—to that extent, at least, they are feminine, and still nourished by the milk of their mothers. "Human creatures," says George, borrowing from Weininger, "are never entirely male or entirely female; there are no men, there are no women, but only sexual majorities." Find me an obviously intelligent man, a man free from sentimentality and illusion, a man hard to deceive, a man of the first class, and I'll show you a man with a wide streak of woman in him. Bonaparte had it; Goethe had it; Schopenhauer had it; Bismarck and Lincoln had it; in Shakespeare, if the Freudians are to be believed, it amounted to downright homosexuality. The essential traits and qualities of the male, the hallmarks of the unpolluted masculine, are at the same time the hallmarks of the *Schafskopf*. The caveman is all muscles and mush. Without a woman to rule him and think for him, he is a truly lamentable spectacle: a baby with whiskers, a rabbit with the frame of an aurochs, a feeble and preposterous caricature of God.

It would be an easy matter, indeed, to demonstrate that superior talent in man is practically always accompanied by this feminine flavour—that complete masculinity and stupidity are often indistinguishable. Lest I be misunderstood I hasten to add that I do not mean to say that masculinity contributes nothing to the complex of chemico-physiological reactions which produces what we call talent; all I mean to say is that this complex is impossible without the feminine contribution—that it is a product of the interplay of the two elements. In women of genius we see the opposite picture. They are commonly distinctly mannish, and shave as well as shine. Think of George Sand, Catherine the Great, Elizabeth of England, Rosa Bonheur, Teresa Carreño or Cosima Wagner. The truth is that neither sex, without some fertilization by the complementary characters of the other, is capable of the highest reaches of human endeavour. Man, without a saving touch of woman in him, is too doltish, too naïve and romantic, too easily deluded and lulled to sleep by his imagination to be anything above a cavalryman, a theologian or a bank director. And woman, without some trace of that divine innocence which is masculine, is too harshly the realist for those vast projections of the fancy which lie at the heart of what we call genius. Here, as elsewhere in the universe, the best effects are obtained by a mingling of elements. The wholly manly man lacks the wit necessary to give objective form to his soaring and secret dreams, and the wholly womanly woman is apt to be too cynical a creature to dream at all.

3. The Masculine Bag of Tricks

WHAT MEN, in their egoism, constantly mistake for a deficiency of intelligence in woman is merely an incapacity for mastering that mass of small intellectual tricks, that complex of petty knowledges, that collection of cerebral rubber-stamps, which constitutes the chief mental equipment of the average male. A man thinks that he is more intelligent than his wife because he can add up a column of figures more accurately, and because he understands the imbecile jargon of the stock market, and because he is able to distinguish between the ideas of rival politicians, and because he is privy to the minutiae of some sordid and degrading business or profession, say soap-selling or the law. But these empty talents, of course, are not really signs of a profound intelligence; they are, in fact, merely superficial accomplishments, and their acquirement puts little more strain on the mental powers than a chimpanzee suffers in learning how to catch a penny or scratch a match. The whole bag of tricks of the average business man, or even of the average professional man, is inordinately childish. It takes no more actual sagacity to carry on the everyday hawking and haggling of the world, or to ladle out its normal doses of bad medicine and worse law, than it takes to operate a taxicab or fry a pan of fish. No observant person, indeed, can come into close contact with the general run of business and professional men—I confine myself to those who seem to get on in the world, and exclude the admitted failures—without marvelling at their intellectual lethargy, their incurable ingenuousness, their appalling lack of ordinary sense. The late Charles Francis Adams, a grandson of one American President and a great-grandson of another, after a long lifetime in intimate association with some of the chief business "geniuses" of that paradise of traders and usurers, the United States, reported in his old age that he had never heard a single one of them say anything worth hearing. These were vigorous and masculine men, and in a man's world they were successful men, but intellectually they were all blank cartridges.

There is, indeed, fair ground for arguing that, if men of that kidney were genuinely intelligent, they would never succeed at their gross and drivelling concerns—that their very capacity to master and retain such balderdash as constitutes their stock in trade is proof of their inferior mentality. The notion is certainly supported by the familiar incompetency of first-rate men for what are called practical concerns. One could not think of Aristotle or Beethoven multiplying 3,472,701 by 99,999 without making a mistake, nor could one think of him remembering the range of this or that railway share for two years, or the number of ten-penny nails in a hundredweight, or the freight on lard from Galveston to Rotterdam. And by the same token one could not imagine him expert at billiards, or at grouse-shooting, or at golf, or at any other of the idiotic games at which what are called successful men commonly divert themselves. In his great study of British genius, Havelock Ellis found that an incapacity for such petty expertness was visible in almost all first-rate men. They are bad at tying cravats. They do not understand the fashionable card-games. They are puzzled by book-keeping. They know nothing of party politics. In brief, they are inert and impotent in the very fields of endeavour that see the average men's highest performances, and are easily surpassed by men who, in actual intelligence, are about as far below them as the *Simidae*.

This lack of skill at manual and mental tricks of a trivial character—which must inevitably appear to a barber or a dentist as stupidity, and to a successful haberdasher as downright imbecility—is a character that men of the first class share with women of the first, second and even third classes. There is at the bottom of it, in truth, something unmistakably feminine; its appearance in a man is almost invariably accompanied by the other touch of femaleness that I have described. Nothing, indeed, could be plainer than the fact that women, as a class, are sadly deficient in the small expertness of men as a class. One seldom, if ever, hears of them succeeding in the occupations which bring out such expertness most lavishly—for example, tuning pianos, repairing clocks, practising law, (*i. e.,* matching petty tricks with some other lawyer), painting portraits, keeping books, or managing factories—despite the circumstance that the great majority of such occupations are well within their physical powers, and that few of them offer any very formidable social barriers to female entrance. There is no external reason why women shouldn't succeed as operative surgeons; the way is wide open, the rewards are large, and there is a special demand for them on grounds of modesty. Nevertheless, not many women graduates in medicine undertake surgery and it is rare for one of them to make a success of it. There is, again, no external reason why women should not prosper at the bar, or as editors of newspapers, or as managers of the lesser sort of factories, or in the wholesale trade, or as hotel-keepers. The taboos that stand in the way are of very small force; various adventurous women have defied them with impunity; once the door is entered there remains no special handicap within. But, as every one knows, the number of women actually practising these trades and professions is very small, and few of them have attained to any distinction in competition with men.

4. Why Women Fail

THE CAUSE thereof, as I say, is not external, but internal. It lies in the same disconcerting apprehension of the larger realities, the same impatience with the paltry and meretricious, the same disqualification for mechanical routine and empty technic which one finds in the higher varieties of men. Even in the pursuits which, by the custom of Christendom, are especially their own, women seldom show any of that elaborately conventionalized and half automatic proficiency which is the pride and boast of most men. It is a commonplace of observation, indeed, that a housewife who actually knows how to cook, or who can make her own clothes with enough skill to conceal the fact from the most casual glance, or who is competent to instruct her children in the elements of morals, learning and hygiene—it is a platitude that such a woman is very rare indeed, and that when she is encountered she is not usually esteemed for her general intelligence. This is particularly true in the United States, where the position of women is higher than in any other civilized or semi-civilized country, and the old assumption of their intellectual inferiority has been most successfully challenged. The American dinner-table, in truth, becomes a monument to the defective technic of the American housewife. The guest who respects his oesophagus, invited to feed upon its discordant and ill-prepared victuals, evades the experience as long and as often as he can, and resigns himself to it as he might resign himself to being shaved by a paralytic. Nowhere else in the world have women more leisure and freedom to improve their minds, and nowhere else do they show a higher level of intelligence, or take part more effectively in affairs of the first importance. But nowhere else is there worse cooking in the home, or a more inept handling of the whole domestic economy, or a larger dependence upon the aid of external substitutes, by men provided, for the skill that is wanting where it theoretically exists. It is surely no mere coincidence that the land of the emancipated and enthroned woman is also the land of canned soup, of canned pork and beans, of whole meals in cans, and of everything else ready-made. And nowhere else is there a more striking tendency to throw the whole business of training the minds of children upon professional teachers, and the whole business of instructing them in morals and religion upon so-called Sunday-schools, and the whole business of developing and caring for their bodies upon playground experts, sex hygienists and other such professionals, most of them mountebanks.

In brief, women rebel—often unconsciously, sometimes even submitting all the while—against the dull, mechanical tricks of the trade that the present organization of society compels them to practise for a living, and that rebellion testifies to their intelligence. If they enjoyed and took pride in those tricks, and showed it by diligence and skill, they would be on all fours with such men as are head waiters, ladies' tailors, schoolmasters or carpet-beaters, and proud of it. The inherent tendency of any woman above the most stupid is to evade the whole obligation, and, if she cannot actually evade it, to reduce its demands to the minimum. And when some accident purges her, either temporarily or permanently, of the inclination to marriage (of which much more anon), and she enters into competition with men in the general business of the world, the sort of career that she commonly carves out offers additional evidence of her mental peculiarity. In whatever calls for no more than an invariable technic and a feeble chicanery she usually fails; in whatever calls for independent thought and resourcefulness· she usually succeeds. Thus she is almost always a failure as a lawyer, for the law requires only an armament of hollow phrases and stereotyped formulae, and a mental habit which puts these phantasms above sense, truth and justice; and she is almost always a failure in business, for business, in the main, is so foul a compound of trivialities and rogueries that her sense of intellectual integrity revolts against it. But she is usually a success as a sick-nurse, for that profession requires ingenuity, quick comprehension, courage in the face of novel and disconcerting situations, and above all, a capacity for penetrating and dominating character;

and whenever she comes into competition with men in the arts, particularly on those secondary planes where simple nimbleness of mind is unaided by the master strokes of genius, she holds her own invariably. The best and most intellectual—*i. e.,* most original and enterprising—play-actors are not men, but women, and so are the best teachers and blackmailers, and a fair share of the best writers, and public functionaries, and executants of music. In the *demimonde* one will find enough acumen and daring, and enough resilience in the face of special difficulties, to put the equipment of any exclusively male profession to shame. If the work of the average man required half the mental agility and readiness of resource of the work of the average prostitute, the average man would be constantly on the verge of starvation.

5. *The Thing Called Intuition*

MEN, AS EVERY one knows, are disposed to question this superior intelligence of women; their egoism demands the denial, and they are seldom reflective enough to dispose of it by logical and evidential analysis. Moreover, as we shall see a bit later on, there is a certain specious appearance of soundness in their position; they have forced upon women an artificial character which well conceals their real character, and women have found it profitable to encourage the deception. But though every normal man thus cherishes the soothing unction that he is the intellectual superior of all women, and particularly of his wife, he constantly gives the lie to his pretension by consulting and deferring to what he calls her intuition. That is to say, he knows by experience that her judgment in many matters of capital concern is more subtle and searching than his own, and, being disinclined to accredit this greater sagacity to a more competent intelligence, he takes refuge behind the doctrine that it is due to some impenetrable and intangible talent for guessing correctly, some half mystical supersense, some vague (and, in essence, infra-human) instinct.

The true nature of this alleged instinct, however, is revealed by an examination of the situations which inspire a man to call it to his aid. These situations do not arise out of the purely technical problems that are his daily concern, but out of the rarer and more fundamental, and hence enormously more difficult problems which beset him only at long and irregular intervals, and so offer a test, not of his mere capacity for being drilled, but of his capacity for genuine ratiocination. No man, I take it, save one consciously inferior and hen-pecked, would consult his wife about hiring a clerk, or about extending credit to some paltry customer, or about some routine piece of tawdry swindling; but not even the most egoistic man would fail to sound the sentiment of his wife about taking a partner into his business, or about standing for public

office, or about combating unfair and ruinous competition, or about marrying off their daughter. Such things
are of massive importance; they lie at the foundation
of well-being; they call for the best thought that the
man confronted by them can muster; the perils hidden
in a wrong decision overcome even the clamours of
vanity. It is in such situations that the superior mental
grasp of women is of obvious utility, and has to be
admitted. It is here that they rise above the insignificant
sentimentalities, superstitions and formulae of men,
and apply to the business their singular talent for
separating the appearance from the substance, and so
exercise what is called their intuition.

Intuition? With all respect, bosh! Then it was intuition that led Darwin to work out the hypothesis of
natural selection. Then it was intuition that fabricated
the gigantically complex score of "Die Walküre." Then
it was intuition that convinced Columbus of the existence of land to the west of the Azores. All this intuition of which so much transcendental rubbish is
merchanted is no more and no less than intelligence—
intelligence so keen that it can penetrate to the hidden
truth through the most formidable wrappings of false
semblance and demeanour, and so little corrupted by
sentimental prudery that it is equal to the even more
difficult task of hauling that truth out into the light,
in all its naked hideousness. Women decide the larger
questions of life correctly and quickly, not because they
are lucky guessers, not because they are divinely inspired, not because they practise a magic inherited
from savagery, but simply and solely because they have

sense. They see at a glance what most men could not see with searchlights and telescopes; they are at grips with the essentials of a problem before men have finished debating its mere externals. They are the supreme realists of the race. Apparently illogical, they are the possessors of a rare and subtle super-logic. Apparently whimsical, they hang to the truth with a tenacity which carries them through every phase of its incessant, jelly-like shifting of form. Apparently unobservant and easily deceived, they see with bright and horrible eyes. . . . In men, too, the same merciless perspicacity sometimes shows itself—men recognized to be more aloof and uninflammable than the general—men of special talent for the logical—sardonic men, cynics. Men, too, sometimes have brains. But that is a rare, rare man, I venture, who is as steadily intelligent, as constantly sound in judgment, as little put off by appearances, as the average women of forty-eight.

II
THE
WAR
BETWEEN
THE
SEXES

6. *How Marriages Are Arranged*

I HAVE SAID that women are not sentimental, *i.e.*, not prone to permit mere emotion and illusion to corrupt their estimation of a situation. The doctrine, perhaps, will raise a protest. The theory that they are is itself a favourite sentimentality, one sentimentality will be brought up to substantiate another; dog will eat dog. But an appeal to a few obvious facts will be enough to sustain my contention, despite the vast accumulation of romantic rubbish to the contrary.

Turn, for example, to the field in which the two sexes come most constantly into conflict, and in which, as a result, their habits of mind are most clearly contrasted—to the field, to wit, of monogamous marriage.

Surely no long argument is needed to demonstrate the superior competence and effectiveness of women here, and therewith their greater self-possession, their saner weighing of considerations, their higher power of resisting emotional suggestion. The very fact that marriages occur at all is a proof, indeed, that they are more cool-headed than men, and more adept in employing their intellectual resources, for it is plainly to a man's interest to avoid marriage as long as possible, and as plainly to a woman's interest to make a favourable marriage as soon as she can. The efforts of the two sexes are thus directed, in one of the capital concerns of life, to diametrically antagonistic ends. Which side commonly prevails? I leave the verdict to the jury. All normal men fight the thing off; some men are successful for relatively long periods; a few extraordinarily intelligent and courageous men (or perhaps lucky ones) escape altogether. But, taking one generation with another, as every one knows, the average man is duly married and the average woman gets a husband. Thus the great majority of women, in this clear-cut and endless conflict, make manifest their substantial superiority to the great majority of men.

Not many men, worthy of the name, gain anything of net value by marriage, at least as the institution is now met with in Christendom. Even assessing its benefits at their most inflated worth, they are plainly overborne by crushing disadvantages. When a man marries it is no more than a sign that the feminine talent for persuasion and intimidation—*i. e.,* the feminine talent for survival in a world of clashing concepts and desires, the feminine competence and intelligence—has forced him into a more or less abhorrent compromise with his own honest inclinations and best interests. Whether that compromise be a sign of his relative stupidity or of his relative cowardice it is all one: the two things, in their symptoms and effects, are almost identical. In the first case he marries because he has been clearly bowled over in a combat of wits; in the second he resigns himself to marriage as the safest form of liaison. In both cases his inherent sentimentality is the chief weapon in the hand of his opponent. It makes him cherish the fiction of his enterprise, and even of his daring, in the midst of the most crude and obvious operations against him. It makes him accept as real the bold play-acting that women always excel at, and at no time more than when stalking a man. It makes him, above all, see a glamour of romance in a transaction which, even at its best, contains almost as much gross trafficking, at bottom, as the sale of a mule.

A man in full possession of the modest faculties that nature commonly apportions to him is at least far enough above idiocy to realize that marriage is a bargain in which he gets the worse of it, even when, in some detail or other, he makes a visible gain. He never, I believe, wants *all* that the thing offers and implies. He wants, at most, no more than certain parts. He may desire, let us say, a housekeeper to protect his goods and entertain his friends—but he may shrink from the thought of sharing his bathtub with any one, and home cooking may be downright poisonous to him. He may yearn for a son to pray at his tomb—and yet suffer acutely at the mere approach of relatives-in-law. He may dream of a beautiful and complaisant mistress, less exigent and mercurial than any a bachelor may hope to discover—and stand aghast at admitting her to his bank-book, his family-tree and his secret ambitions. He may want company and not intimacy, or intimacy and not company. He may want a cook and not a partner in his business, or a partner in his business and not a cook. But in order to get the precise thing or things that he wants, he has to take a lot of other things that he doesn't want—that no sane man, in truth, could imaginably want—and it is to the enterprise of forcing him into this almost Armenian bargain that the woman of his "choice" addresses herself. Once the game is fairly set, she searches out his weaknesses with the utmost delicacy and accuracy, and plays upon them with all her superior resources. He carries a handicap from the start. His sentimental and unintelligent belief in theories that she knows quite well are not true —*e. g.,* the theory that she shrinks from him, and is modestly appalled by the banal carnalities of marriage itself—gives her a weapon against him which she drives home with instinctive and compelling art. The moment she discerns this sentimentality bubbling within him—that is, the moment his oafish smirks and eye-rollings signify that he has achieved the intellectual disaster that is called falling in love—he is hers to do with as she will. Save for acts of God, he is forthwith as good as married.

7. *The Feminine Attitude*

THIS SENTIMENTALITY in marriage is seldom, if ever, observed in women. For reasons that we shall examine later, they have much more to gain by the business than men, and so they are prompted by their cooler sagacity to enter upon it on the most favourable terms possible, and with the minimum admixture of disarming emotion. Men almost invariably get their mates by the process called falling in love; save among the aristocracies of the North and Latin men, the marriage of convenience is relatively rare; a hundred men marry "beneath" them to every woman who perpetrates the same folly. And what is meant by this so-called falling in love? What is meant by it is a procedure whereby a man accounts for the fact of his marriage, after feminine initiative and generalship have made it inevitable, by enshrouding it in a purple maze of romance—in brief, by setting up the doctrine that an obviously self-possessed and mammalian woman, engaged deliberately in the most important adventure of her life, and with the keenest understanding of its utmost implications, is a naïve, tender, moony and almost disembodied creature, enchanted and made perfect by a passion that has stolen

upon her unawares, and which she could not acknowledge, even to herself, without blushing to death. By
this preposterous doctrine, the defeat and enslavement
of the man is made glorious, and even gifted with a
touch of flattering naughtiness. The sheer horsepower
of his wooing has assailed and overcome her maiden
modesty; she trembles in his arms; he has been granted
a free franchise to work his wicked will upon her.
Thus do the ambulant images of God cloak their
shackles proudly, and divert the judicious with their
boastful shouts.

Women, it is almost needless to point out, are much
more cautious about embracing the conventional hocus-
pocus of the situation. They never acknowledge that
they have fallen in love, as the phrase is, until the man
has formally avowed the delusion, and so cut off his
retreat; to do otherwise would be to bring down upon
their heads the mocking and contumely of all their
sisters. With them, falling in love thus appears in the
light of an afterthought, or, perhaps more accurately,
in the light of a contagion. The theory, it would seem,
is that the love of the man, laboriously avowed, has
inspired it instantly, and by some unintelligible magic;
that it was non-existent until the heat of his own flames
set it off. This theory, it must be acknowledged, has a
certain element of fact in it. A woman seldom allows
herself to be swayed by emotion while the principal
business is yet afoot and its issue still in doubt; to do
so would be to expose a degree of imbecility that is
confined only to the half-wits of the sex. But once the
man is definitely committed, she frequently unbends a

bit, if only as a relief from the strain of a fixed purpose, and so, throwing off her customary inhibitions, she indulges in the luxury of a more or less forced and mawkish sentiment. It is, however, almost unheard of for her to permit herself this relaxation before the sentimental intoxication of the man is assured. To do otherwise—that is, to confess, even *post facto,* to an anterior descent,—would expose her, as I have said, to the scorn of all other women. Such a confession would be an admission that emotion had got the better of her at a critical intellectual moment, and in the eyes of women, as in the eyes of the small minority of genuinely intelligent men, no treason to the higher cerebral centres could be more disgraceful.

8. The Male Beauty

THIS DISDAIN of sentimental weakness, even in those higher reaches where it is mellowed by æsthetic sensibility, is well revealed by the fact that women are seldom bemused by mere beauty in men. Save on the stage, the handsome fellow has no appreciable advantage in amour over his more Gothic brother. In real life, indeed, he is viewed with the utmost suspicion by all women save the most stupid. In him the vanity native to his sex is seen to

mount to a degree that is positively intolerable. It not
only irritates by its very nature; it also throws about
him a sort of unnatural armour, and so makes him
resistant to the ordinary approaches. For this reason,
the matrimonial enterprises of the more reflective and
analytical sort of women are almost always directed to
men whose lack of pulchritude makes them easier to
bring down, and, what is more important still, easier
to hold down. The weight of opinion among women
is decidedly against the woman who falls in love with
an Apollo. She is regarded, at best, as a flighty creature,
and at worst, as one pushing bad taste to the verge of
indecency. Such weaknesses are resigned to women
approaching senility, and to the more ignoble variety
of women labourers. A shop girl, perhaps, may plaus-
ibly fall in love with a moving-picture actor, and a
half-idiotic old widow may succumb to a youth with
shoulders like the Parthenon, but no woman of poise
and self-respect, even supposing her to be transiently
flustered by a lovely buck, would yield to that madness
for an instant, or confess it to her dearest friend.
Women know how little such purely superficial values
are worth. The voice of their order, the first taboo of
their freemasonry, is firmly against making a sentimental debauch of the serious business of marriage.

This disdain of the pretty fellow is often accounted
for by amateur psychologists on the ground that women
are anæsthetic to beauty—that they lack the quick
and delicate responsiveness of man. Nothing could be
more absurd. Women, in point of fact, commonly
have a far keener æsthetic sense than men. Beauty

is more important to them; they give more thought
to it; they crave more of it in their immediate sur-
roundings. The average man, at least in England and
America, takes a sort of bovine pride in his anæsthesia
to the arts; he can think of them only as sources of
tawdry and somewhat discreditable amusement; one
seldom hears of him showing half the enthusiasm for
any beautiful thing that his wife displays in the
presence of a fine fabric, an effective colour, or a graceful form, say in millinery. The truth is that women are
resistant to so-called beauty in men for the simple and
sufficient reason that such beauty is chiefly imaginary.
A truly beautiful man, indeed, is as rare as a truly
beautiful piece of jewelry. What men mistake for
beauty in themselves is usually nothing save a certain
hollow gaudiness, a revolting flashiness, the superficial
splendour of a prancing animal. The most lovely moving-picture actor, considered in the light of genuine
æsthetic values, is no more than a piece of vulgarity;
his like is to be found, not in the Uffizi gallery or
among the harmonies of Brahms, but among the plush
sofas, rococo clocks and hand-painted oil-paintings of
a third-rate auction-room. All women, save the least
intelligent, penetrate this imposture with sharp eyes.
They know that the human body, except for a brief
time in infancy, is not a beautiful thing, but a hideous
thing. Their own bodies give them no delight; it is
their constant effort to disguise and conceal them;
they never expose them æsthetically, but only as an act
of the grossest sexual provocation. If it were advertised
that a troupe of men of easy virtue were to appear

half-clothed upon a public stage, exposing their chests, thighs, arms and calves, the only women who would go to the entertainment would be a few delayed adolescents, a psychopathic old maid or two, and a guard of indignant members of the parish Ladies Aid Society.

9. Men as Æsthetes

MEN SHOW no such sagacious apprehension of the relatively feeble loveliness of the human frame. The most effective lure that a woman can hold out to a man is the lure of what he fatuously conceives to be her beauty. This so-called beauty, of course, is almost always a pure illusion. The female body, even at its best, is very defective in form; it has harsh curves and very clumsily distributed masses; compared to it the average milk-jug, or even cuspidor, is a thing of intelligent and gratifying design—in brief, an *objet d'art*. The fact was curiously (and humorously) displayed during the late war, when great numbers of women in all the belligerent countries began putting on uniforms. Instantly they appeared in public in their grotesque burlesques of the official garb of aviators, elevator boys, bus conductors, train guards, and so on, their deplorable deficiency in design was unescapably revealed. A man, save he be fat, *i. e.,* of womanish contours, usually looks better in uniform than in mufti; the tight lines set off his figure. But a woman is at once given away: she looks like a dumbbell run over by an express train. Below the neck by the bow and below the waist astern there are two masses that simply refuse to fit into a balanced composition. Viewed from the side, she presents an exaggerated S bisected by an imperfect straight line, and so she inevitably suggests a drunken dollar-mark. Her ordinary clothing cunningly conceals this fundamental imperfection. It swathes those impossible masses in draperies soothingly uncertain of outline. But putting her into uniform is like stripping her. Instantly all her alleged beauty vanishes.

Moreover, it is extremely rare to find a woman who shows even the modest sightliness that her sex is theoretically capable of; it is only the rare beauty who is even tolerable. The average woman, until art comes to her aid, is ungraceful, misshapen, badly calved and crudely articulated, even for a woman. If she has a good torso, she is almost sure to be bow-legged. If she has good legs, she is almost sure to have bad teeth. If she has good teeth, she is almost sure to have scrawny hands, or muddy eyes, or hair like oakum, or no chin. A woman who meets fair tests all 'round is so uncommon that she becomes a sort of marvel, and usually gains a livelihood by exhibiting herself as such, either on the stage, in the half-world, or as the private jewel of some wealthy connoisseur.

But this lack of genuine beauty in women lays on them no practical disadvantage in the primary business

of their sex, for its effects are more than overborne by
the emotional suggestibility, the herculean capacity for
illusion, the almost total absence of critical sense of
men. Men do not demand genuine beauty, even in the
most modest doses; they are quite content with the
mere appearance of beauty. That is to say, they show
no talent whatever for differentiating between the artificial and the real. A film of face powder, skilfully
applied, is as satisfying to them as an epidermis of
damask. The hair of a dead Chinaman, artfully dressed
and dyed, gives them as much delight as the authentic
tresses of Venus. A false hip intrigues them as effectively as the soundest one of living fascia. A pretty
frock fetches them quite as surely and securely as
lovely legs, shoulders, hands or eyes. In brief, they
estimate women, and hence acquire their wives, by
reckoning up purely superficial aspects, which is just as
intelligent as estimating an egg by purely superficial
aspects. They never go behind the returns; it never oc-
curs to them to analyze the impressions they receive.
The result is that many a man, deceived by such paltry
sophistications, never really sees his wife—that is, as
God is supposed to see her, and as the embalmer will
see her—until they have been married for years. All
the tricks may be infantile and obvious, but in the face
of so naïve a spectator the temptation to continue practising them is irresistible. A trained nurse tells me that
even when undergoing the extreme discomforts of
parturition the great majority of women continue to
modify their complexions with pulverized talcs, and to
give thought to the arrangement of their hair. Such

transparent devices, to be sure, reduce the psychologist to a sour sort of mirth, and yet it must be plain that they suffice to entrap and make fools of men, even the most discreet. I know of no man, indeed, who is wholly resistant to female beauty, and I know of no man, even among those engaged professionally by æsthetic problems, who habitually and automatically distinguishes the genuine from the imitation. He may do it now and then; he may even preen himself upon his unusual discrimination; but given the right woman and the right stage setting, and he will be deceived almost as readily as a yokel fresh from the cabbage-field.

10. The Process of Delusion

Such poor fools, rolling their eyes in appraisement of such meagre female beauty as is on display in Christendom, bring to their judgments a capacity but slightly greater than that a cow would bring to the estimation of epistemologies. They are so unfitted for the business that they are even unable to agree upon its elements. Let one such man succumb to the plaster charms of some prancing miss, and all his friends will wonder what is the matter with him. No two are in accord as to which is the most beautiful woman in their own town or street. Turn six of

them loose in a millinery shop or the parlour of a bordello, and there will be no dispute whatsoever; each will
offer the crown of love and beauty to a different girl.

And what æsthetic deafness, dumbness and blind-
ness thus open the way for, vanity instantly reinforces.
That is to say, once a normal man has succumbed to
the meretricious charms of a definite fair one (or, more
accurately, once a definite fair one has marked him
out and grabbed him by the nose), he defends his
choice with all the heat and steadfastness appertaining
to the defense of a point of the deepest honour. To tell
a man flatly that his wife is not beautiful, or even that
his stenographer or manicurist is not beautiful, is so
harsh and intolerable an insult to his taste that even an
enemy seldom ventures upon it. One would offend
him far less by arguing that his wife is an idiot. One
would, relatively speaking, almost caress him by spitting
into his eye. The ego of the male is simply unable to
stomach such an affront. It is a weapon as discreditable as the poison of the Borgias.

Thus, on humane grounds, a conspiracy of silence
surrounds the delusion of female beauty, and so its
victim is permitted to get quite as much delight out
of it as if it were sound. The baits he swallows most
are not edible and nourishing baits, but simply bright
and gaudy ones. He succumbs to a pair of well-man-
aged eyes, a graceful twist of the body, a synthetic
complexion or a skilful display of ankles without giving the slightest thought to the fact that a whole
woman is there, and that within the cranial cavity of

the woman lies a brain, and that the idiosyncrasies of
that brain are of vastly more importance than all imaginable physical stigmata combined. Those idiosyncrasies may make for amicable relations in the
complex and difficult bondage called marriage; they
may, on the contrary, make for joustings of a downright impossible character. But not many men, lost
in the emotional maze preceding, are capable of any
very clear examination of such facts. The truth is that
they dodge the facts, even when they are favourable,
and lay all stress upon the surrounding and concealing
superficialities. The average stupid and sentimental
man, if he has a noticeably sensible wife, is almost
apologetic about it. The ideal of his sex is always a
pretty wife, and the vanity and coquetry that so often
go with prettiness are erected into charms. In other
words, men play the love game so unintelligently that
they often esteem a woman in proportion as she seems
to disdain and make a mock of her intelligence.
Women seldom, if ever, make that blunder. What they
commonly value in a man is not mere showiness,
whether physical or spiritual, but that compound of
small capacities which makes up masculine efficiency
and passes for masculine intelligence. This intelligence,
at its highest, has a human value substantially equal
to that of their own. In a man's world it at least gets its
definite rewards; it guarantees security, position, a
livelihood; it is a commodity that is merchantable.
Women thus accord it a certain respect, and esteem it
in their husbands, and so seek it out.

11. Biological Considerations

O FAR AS I can make
out by experiments on laboratory animals and by such
discreet vivisections as are possible under our laws,
there is no biological necessity for the superior acumen
and circumspection of women. That is to say, it does
not lie in any anatomical or physiological advantage.
The essential feminine machine is no better than the
essential masculine machine; both are monuments to
the maladroitness of a much over-praised Creator.
Women, it would seem, actually have smaller brains
than men, though perhaps not in proportion to weight.
Their nervous responses, if anything, are a bit duller
than those of men; their muscular co-ordinations are
surely no prompter. One finds quite as many obvious
botches among them; they have as many bodily
blemishes; they are infested by the same microscopic
parasites; their senses are as obtuse; their ears stand
out as absurdly. Even assuming that their special
malaises are wholly offset by the effects of alcoholism
in the male, they suffer patently from the same
adenoids, gastritis, cholelithiasis, nephritis, tuberculosis,
carcinoma, arthritis and so on—in short, from the
same disturbances of colloidal equilibrium that pro-

duce religion, delusions of grandeur, democracy, pyaemia, night sweats, the yearning to save humanity, and all other such distempers in men. They have, at bottom, the same weaknesses and appetites. They react in substantially the same way to all chemical and mechanical agents. A dose of hydrocyanic acid, administered *per ora* to the most sagacious woman imaginable, affects her just as swiftly and just as deleteriously as it affects a tragedian, a crossing-sweeper, or an ambassador to the Court of St. James. And once a bottle of Côte Rôtie or Scharlachberger is in her, even the least emotional woman shows the same complex of sentimentalities that a man shows, and is as maudlin and idiotic as he is.

Nay; the superior acumen and self-possession of women is not inherent in any peculiarity of their constitutions, and above all, not in any advantage of a purely physical character. Its springs are rather to be sought in a physical *dis*advantage—that is, in the mechanical inferiority of their frames, their relative lack of tractive capacity, their deficiency as brute engines. That deficiency, as every one knows, is partly a direct heritage from those females of the *Pongo pygmaeus* who were their probable fore-runners in the world; the same thing is to be observed in the females of almost all other species of mammals. But it is also partly due to the effects of use under civilization, and, above all, to what evolutionists call sexual selection. In other words, women were already measurably weaker than men at the dawn of human history, and that relative weakness has been progressively augmented in the interval by the conditions of human life. For one thing, the process of bringing forth young has become so much more exhausting as refinement has replaced savage sturdiness and callousness, and the care of them in infancy has become so much more onerous as the growth of cultural complexity has made education more intricate, that the two functions now lay vastly heavier burdens upon the strength and attention of a woman than they lay upon the strength and attention of any other female. And for another thing, the consequent disability and need of physical protection, by feeding and inflaming the already large vanity of man, have caused him to attach a concept of attractiveness to feminine weakness, so that he has come to esteem his woman, not in proportion as she is self-sufficient as a social animal but in proportion as she is dependent. In this vicious circle of influences women have been caught, and as a result their chief physical character today is their fragility. A woman cannot lift as much as a man. She cannot walk as far. She cannot exert as much mechanical energy in any other way. Even her alleged superior endurance, as Havelock Ellis has demonstrated in "Man and Woman," is almost wholly mythical; she cannot, in point of fact, stand nearly so much hardship as a man can stand, and so the law, usually an ass, exhibits an unaccustomed accuracy of observation in its assumption that, whenever husband and wife are exposed alike to fatal suffering, say in a shipwreck, the wife dies first.

So far we have been among platitudes. There is less of overt platitude in the doctrine that it is precisely this physical frailty that has given women their peculiar nimbleness and effectiveness on the intellectual side. Nevertheless, it is equally true. What they have done is what every healthy and elastic organism does in like case; they have sought compensation for their impotence in one field by employing their resources in another field to the utmost, and out of that constant and maximum use has come a marked enlargement of those resources. On the one hand the sum of them present in a given woman has been enormously increased by natural selection, so that every woman, so to speak, inherits a certain extramasculine mental dexterity as a mere function of her femaleness. And on the other hand every woman, over and above this almost unescapable legacy from her actual grandmothers, also inherits admission to that traditional wisdom which constitutes the esoteric philosophy of woman as a whole. The virgin at adolescence is thus in the position of an unusually fortunate apprentice, for she is not only naturally gifted but also apprenticed to extraordinarily competent masters. While a boy at the same period is learning from his elders little more than a few empty technical tricks, a few paltry vices and a few degrading enthusiasms, his sister is under instruction in all those higher exercises of the wits that her special deficiencies make necessary to her security, and in particular in all those exercises which aim at overcoming the physi-

cal, and hence social and economic superiority of man
by attacks upon his inferior capacity for clear reasoning, uncorrupted by illusion and sentimentality.

12. Honour

ERE, IT IS obvious, the
process of intellectual development takes colour from
the *Sklavenmoral,* and is, in a sense, a product of it.
The Jews, as Nietzsche has demonstrated, got their unusual intelligence by the same process; a contrary
process is working in the case of the English and the
Americans, and has begun to show itself in the case of
the French and Germans. The sum of feminine wisdom that I have just mentioned—the body of feminine
devices and competences that is handed down from
generation to generation of women—is, in fact, made
up very largely of doctrines and expedients that in-
fallibly appear to the average sentimental man, helpless as he is before them, as cynical and immoral. He
commonly puts this aversion into the theory that women have no sense of honour. The criticism, of course,
is characteristically banal. Honour is a concept too
tangled to be analyzed here, but it may be sufficient
to point out that it is predicated upon a feeling of
absolute security, and that, in that capital conflict be-

tween man and woman out of which rises most of
man's complaint of its absence—to wit, the conflict
culminating in marriage, already described—the security
of the woman is not something that is in actual being,
but something that she is striving with all arms to
attain. In such a conflict it must be manifest that
honour can have no place. An animal fighting for its
very existence uses all possible means of offence and
defence, however foul. Even man, for all his boasting
about honour, seldom displays it when he has anything
of the first value at hazard. He is honourable, perhaps, in gambling, for gambling is a mere vice, but
it is quite unusual for him to be honourable in business, for business is bread and butter. He is honourable
(so long as the stake is trivial) in his sports, but he
seldom permits honour to interfere with his perjuries
in a lawsuit, or with hitting below the belt in any other
sort of combat that is in earnest. The history of all his
wars is a history of mutual allegations of dishonourable practices, and such allegations are nearly always
well grounded. The best imitation of honour that he
ever actually achieves in them is a highly self-conscious
sentimentality which prompts him to be humane to
the opponent who has been wounded, or disarmed, or
otherwise made innocuous. Even here his so-called
honour is little more than a form of play-acting, both
maudlin and dishonest. In the actual death-struggle
he invariably bites.

Perhaps one of the chief charms of woman lies precisely in the fact that they are dishonourable, *i. e.,* that
they are relatively uncivilized. In the midst of all the

puerile repressions and inhibitions that hedge them round, they continue to show a gipsy spirit. No genuine woman ever gives a hoot for law if law happens to stand in the way of her private interest. She is essentially an outlaw, a rebel, what H. G. Wells calls a nomad. The boons of civilization are so noisily cried up by sentimentalists that we are all apt to overlook its disadvantages. Intrinsically, it is a mere device for regimenting men. Its perfect symbol is the goose-step. The most civilized man is simply that man who has been most successful in caging and harnessing his honest and natural instincts—that is, the man who has done most cruel violence to his own ego in the interest of the commonweal. The value of this commonweal is always overestimated. What is it at bottom? Simply the greatest good to the greatest number—of petty rogues, ignoramuses and poltroons.

The capacity for submitting to and prospering comfortably under this cheese-monger's civilization is far more marked in men than in women, and far more in inferior men than in men of the higher categories. It must be obvious to even so pathetic an ass as a university professor of history that very few of the genuinely first-rate men of the race have been wholly civilized, in the sense that the term is employed in newspapers and in the pulpit. Think of Caesar, Bonaparte, Luther, Frederick the Great, Cromwell, Barbarossa, Innocent III, Bolivar, Hannibal, Alexander, and to come down to our own time, Grant, Stonewall Jackson, Bismarck, Wagner, Garibaldi and Cecil Rhodes.

THE FACT that women have a greater capacity than men for controlling and concealing their emotions is not an indication that they are *more* civilized, but a proof that they are *less* civilized. This capacity, so rare today, and withal so valuable and worthy of respect, is a characteristic of savages, not of civilized men, and its loss is one of the penalties that the race has paid for the tawdry boon of civilization. Your true savage, reserved, dignified, and courteous, knows how to mask his feelings, even in the face of the most desperate assault upon them; your civilized man is forever yielding to them. Civilization, in fact, grows more and more maudlin and hysterical; especially under democracy it tends to degenerate into a mere combat of crazes; the whole aim of practical politics is to keep the populace alarmed (and hence clamorous to be led to safety) by an endless series of hobgoblins, most of them imaginary. Wars are no longer waged by the will of superior men, capable of judging dispassionately and intelligently the causes behind them and the effects flowing out of them. They are now begun by first throwing a mob into a panic;

they are ended only when it has spent its ferine fury. Here the effect of civilization has been to reduce the noblest of the arts, once the repository of an exalted etiquette and the chosen avocation of the very best men of the race, to the level of a riot of peasants. All the wars of Christendom are now disgusting and degrading; the conduct of them has passed out of the hands of nobles and knights and into the hands of mob-orators, money-lenders, and atrocity-mongers. To recreate one's self with war in the grand manner, as Prince Eugene, Marlborough and the Old Dessauer knew it, one must now go among barbarian peoples.

Women are nearly always against war in modern times, for the reasons brought forward to justify it are usually either transparently dishonest or childishly sentimental, and hence provoke their scorn. But once the business is begun, they commonly favour its conduct *à outrance,* and are thus in accord with the theory of the great captains of more spacious days. In Germany, during the late war, the protests against the *Schrecklichkeit* practised by the imperial army and navy did not come from women, but from sentimental men; in England and the United States there is no record that any woman ever raised her voice against the blockade which destroyed hundreds of thousands of German children. I was on both sides of the bloody chasm during the war, and I cannot recall meeting a single woman who subscribed to the puerile doctrine that, in so vast a combat between nations, there could still be categories of non-combatants, with a right of asylum on armed ships and in garrisoned towns. This imbecility was maintained only by men, large numbers of whom simultaneously took part in wholesale massacres of such non-combatants. The women were superior to such hypocrisy. They recognized the nature of modern war instantly and accurately, and advocated no disingenuous efforts to conceal it.

14. Pseudo-Anæsthesia

THE FEMININE talent for concealing emotion is probably largely responsible for the common masculine belief that women are devoid of passion, and contemplate its manifestations in the male with something akin to trembling. Here the talent itself is helped out by the fact that very few masculine observers, on the occasions when they give attention to the matter, are in a state of mind conducive to exact observation. The truth is, of course, that there is absolutely no reason to believe that the normal woman is passionless, or that the minority of women who unquestionably *are* is of formidable dimensions. To be sure, the peculiar vanity of men, particularly in the Northern countries, makes them place a high value upon the virginal type of woman, and so this type tends to grow more common by sexual selection, but despite that fact, it has by no means superseded the normal

type, so realistically described by the theologians and
publicists of the Middle Ages. It would, however, be
rash to assert that this long-continued sexual selection
has not made itself felt, even in the normal type. Its
chief effect, perhaps, is to make it measurably easier for
a woman to conquer and conceal emotion than it is
for a man. But this is a mere reinforcement of a native
quality or, at all events, a quality long antedating the
rise of the curious preference just mentioned. That
preference obviously owes its origin to the concept of
private property and is most evident in those countries
in which the largest proportion of males are property
owners, *i. e.,* in which the property-owning caste reaches
down into the lowest conceivable strata of bounders
and ignoramuses. The low-caste man is never quite
sure of his wife unless he is convinced that she is entirely devoid of amorous susceptibility. Thus he grows
uneasy whenever she shows any sign of responding in
kind to his own elephantine emotions, and is apt to
be suspicious of even so trivial a thing as a hearty
response to a connubial kiss. If he could manage to rid
himself of such suspicions, there would be less public
gabble about anæsthetic wives, and fewer books written by quacks with sure cures for them, and a good
deal less cold-mutton formalism and boredom at the
domestic hearth.

I have a feeling that the husband of this sort—he is
very common in the United States, and almost as common among the middle classes of England, Germany
and Scandinavia—does himself a serious disservice, and
that he is uneasily conscious of it. Having got himself

a wife to his austere taste, he finds that she is rather depressing—that his vanity is almost as painfully damaged by her emotional inertness as it would have been by a too provocative and hedonistic spirit. For the thing that chiefly delights a man, when some woman has gone through the solemn buffoonery of yielding to his great love, is the sharp and flattering contrast between her reserve in the presence of other men and her enchanting complaisance in the presence of himself. Here his vanity is enormously tickled. To the world in general she seems remote and unapproachable; to him she is docile, fluttering, gurgling, even a bit abandoned. It is as if some great magnifico male, some inordinate czar or kaiser, should step down from the throne to play dominoes with him behind the door. The greater the contrast between the lady's two fronts, the greater his satisfaction—up to, of course, the point where his suspicions are aroused. Let her diminish that contrast ever so little on the public side—by smiling at a handsome actor, by saying a word too many to an attentive head-waiter, by holding the hand of the rector of the parish, by winking amiably at his brother or at her sister's husband—and at once the poor fellow begins to look for clandestine notes, to employ private inquiry agents, and to scrutinize the eyes, ears, noses and hair of his children with shameful doubts. This explains many domestic catastrophes.

THE MAN-HATING woman, like the cold woman, is largely imaginary. One often encounters references to her in literature, but who has ever met her in real life? As for me, I doubt that such a monster has ever actually existed. There are, of course, women who spend a great deal of time denouncing and reviling men, but these are certainly not genuine man-haters; they are simply women who have done their utmost to snare men, and failed. Of such sort are the majority of inflammatory suffragettes of the sex-hygiene and birth-control species. The rigid limitation of offspring, in fact, is chiefly advocated by women who run no more risk of having unwilling motherhood forced upon them than so many mummies of the Tenth Dynasty. All their unhealthy interest in such noisome matters has behind it merely a subconscious yearning to attract the attention of men, who are supposed to be partial to enterprises that are difficult or forbidden. But certainly the enterprise of dissuading such a propagandist from her gospel would not be difficult, and I know of no law forbidding it.

I'll begin to believe in the man-hater the day I am introduced to a woman who has definitely and finally refused a chance of marriage to a man who is of her own station in life, able to support her, unafflicted by any loathsome disease, and of reasonably decent aspect and manners—in brief a man who is thoroughly eligible. I doubt that any such woman breathes the air of Christendom. Whenever one comes to confidential terms with an unmarried woman, of course, she favours one with a long chronicle of the men she has refused to marry, greatly to their grief. But unsentimental cross-examination, at least in my experience, always develops the fact that every one of these men suffered from some obvious and intolerable disqualification. Either he had a wife already and was vague about his ability to get rid of her, or he was drunk when he was brought to his proposal and repudiated it or forgot it the next day, or he was a bankrupt, or he was old and decrepit, or he was young and plainly idiotic, or he had diabetes or a bad heart, or his relatives were impossible, or he believed in spiritualism, or democracy, or the Baconian theory, or some other such nonsense. Restricting the thing to men palpably eligible, I believe thoroughly that no sane woman has ever actually muffed a chance. Now and then, perhaps, a miraculously fortunate girl has two victims on the mat simultaneously, and has to lose one. But they are seldom, if ever, both *good* chances; one is nearly always a duffer, thrown in in the telling to make the bourgeoisie marvel.

THE REASON why all this has to be stated here is simply that women, who could state it much better, have almost unanimously refrained from discussing such matters at all. One finds, indeed, a sort of general conspiracy, infinitely alert and jealous, against the publication of the esoteric wisdom of the sex, and even against the acknowledgment that any such body of erudition exists at all. Men, having more vanity and less discretion, are a good deal less cautious. There is, in fact, a whole literature of masculine babbling, ranging from Machiavelli's appalling confession of political theory to the egoistic confidences of such men as Nietzsche, Jean Jacques Rousseau, Casanova, Max Stirner, Benvenuto Cellini, Napoleon Bonaparte and Lord Chesterfield. But it is very rarely that a Marie Bashkirtsev or Margot Asquith lets down the veils which conceal the acroamatic doctrine of the other sex. It is transmitted from mother to daughter, so to speak, behind the door. One observes its practical workings, but hears little about its principles. The causes of this secrecy are obvious. Women, in the last analysis, can prevail against men in the great struggle for power and security only by keeping

them disarmed, and, in the main, unwarned. In a
pitched battle, with the devil taking the hindmost,
their physical and economic inferiority would inevitably bring them to disaster. Thus they have to
apply their peculiar talents warily, and with due regard to the danger of arousing the foe. He must be
attacked without any formal challenge, and even without any suspicion of challenge. This strategy lies at the
heart of what Nietzsche called the slave morality—in
brief, a morality based upon a concealment of egoistic
purpose, a code of ethics having for its foremost character a bold denial of its actual aim.

III
MARRIAGE

17. *Fundamental Motives*

How successful such a concealment may be is well displayed by the general acceptance of the notion that women are reluctant to enter into marriage—that they have to be persuaded to it by eloquence and pertinacity, and even by a sort of intimidation. The truth is that, in a world almost divested of intelligible idealism, and hence dominated by a senseless worship of the practical, marriage offers the best career that the average woman can reasonably aspire to, and, in the case of very many women, the only one that actually offers a livelihood. What is esteemed and valuable, in our materialistic and unintelligent society, is precisely that petty practical efficiency at which men are expert, and which serves them in place of free intelligence. A woman, save she show a masculine strain that verges upon the pathological, cannot hope to challenge men in general in this department, but it is always open to her to exchange her sexual charm for a lion's share in the earnings of one man, and this is what she almost invariably tries to do. That is to say, she tries to get a husband, for getting a husband means, in a sense, enslaving an expert, and so covering up her own lack of expertness, and escaping its consequences. Thereafter she has at least one stout line of defence against a struggle for existence in which the prospect of survival is chiefly based, not upon the talents that are typically hers, but upon those that she typically lacks. Before the average woman succumbs in this struggle, some man or other must succumb first. Thus her craft converts her handicap into an advantage.

In this security lies the most important of all the benefits that a woman attains by marriage. It is, in fact, the most important benefit that the mind can imagine, for the whole effort of the human race, under our industrial society, is concentrated upon the attainment of it. But there are other benefits, too. One of them is that increase in dignity which goes with an obvious success; the woman who has got herself a satisfactory husband, or even a highly imperfect husband, is regarded with respect by other women, and has a contemptuous patronage for those who have failed to do likewise. Again, marriage offers her the only safe opportunity, considering the levantine view of women as property which Christianity has pre-

served in our civilization, to obtain gratification for
that powerful complex of instincts which we call the
sexual, and, in particular, for the instinct of maternity.
The woman who has not had a child remains incomplete, ill at ease, and more than a little ridiculous.
She is in the position of a man who has never stood
in battle; she has missed the most colossal experience
of her sex. Moreover, a social odium goes with her
loss. Other women regard her as a sort of permanent
tyro, and treat her with ill-concealed disdain, and
deride the very virtue which lies at the bottom of her
experiential penury. There would seem to be, indeed,
but small respect among women for virginity *per se*.
They are against the woman who has got rid of hers
outside marriage, not because they think she has lost
anything intrinsically valuable, but because she has
made a bad bargain, and one that materially di-
minishes the sentimental respect for virtue held by
men, and hence one against the general advantage
and well-being of the sex. In other words, it is a
guild resentment that they feel, not a moral resentment. Women, in general, are not actively moral,
nor, for that matter, noticeably modest. Every man,
indeed, who is in wide practice among them is occasionally astounded and horrified to discover, on
some rainy afternoon, an almost complete absence of
modesty in some women of the highest respectability.

But of all things that a woman gains by marriage
the most valuable is economic security. Such security,
of course, is seldom absolute, but usually merely rela-

tive: the best provider among husbands may die without enough life insurance, or run off with some
preposterous light of love, or become an invalid or
insane, or step over the intangible and wavering line
which separates business success from a prison cell.
Again, a woman may be deceived: there are stray
women who are credulous and sentimental, and stray
men who are cunning. Yet again, a woman may make
false deductions from evidence accurately before her,
ineptly guessing that the clerk she marries today will
be the head of the firm tomorrow, instead of merely
the bookkeeper tomorrow. But on the whole it must
be plain that a woman, in marrying, usually obtains
for herself a reasonably secure position in that station
of life to which she is accustomed. She seeks a husband, not sentimentally, but realistically: she always
gives thought to the economic situation; she seldom
takes a chance if it is possible to avoid it. It is common for men to marry women who bring nothing to
the joint capital of marriage save good looks and an
appearance of vivacity; it is almost unheard of for
women to neglect more prosaic inquiries. Many a
rich man, at least in America, marries his typist or
the governess of his sister's children and is happy
thereafter, but when a rare woman enters upon a
comparable marriage she is commonly set down as
insane, and the disaster that almost always ensues
quickly confirms the diagnosis.

The economic and social advantage that women
thus seek in marriage—and the seeking is visible no
less in the kitchen wench who aspires to the heart

of a policeman than in the fashionable flapper who looks for a husband with a Rolls-Royce—is, by a curious twist of fate, one of the underlying causes of their precarious economic condition before marriage rescues them. In a civilization which lays its greatest stress upon an uninspired and almost automatic expertness, and offers its highest rewards to the more intricate forms thereof, they suffer the disadvantage of being less capable of it than men. Part of this disadvantage, as we have seen, is congenital; their very intellectual enterprise makes it difficult for them to become the efficient machines that men are. But part of it is also due to the fact that, with marriage always before them, colouring their every vision of the future, and holding out a steady promise of swift and complete relief, they are under no such implacable pressure as men are to acquire the sordid arts they revolt against. The time is too short and the incentive too feeble. Before the woman employé of twenty-one can master a tenth of the idiotic "knowledge" in the head of the male clerk of thirty, or even convince herself that it is worth mastering, she has married the head of the establishment or maybe the clerk himself, and so abandons the business. It is, indeed, not until a woman has definitely put away the hope of marriage, or, at all events, admitted the possibility that she may have to do so soon or late, that she buckles down in earnest to whatever craft she practises, and makes a genuine effort to develop competence. No sane man, seeking a woman for a post requiring laborious training and unremitting diligence, would

select a woman still definitely young and marriage-
able. To the contrary, he would choose either a woman
so unattractive sexually as to be palpably incapable of
snaring a man, or one so embittered by some catas-
trophe of amour as to be pathologically emptied of
the normal aspirations of her sex.

18. The Process of Courtship

THIS BEMUSEMENT of the
typical woman by the notion of marriage has been
noted as self-evident by every literate student of the
phenomena of sex, from the early Christian fathers
down to Nietzsche, Ellis and Shaw. That it is denied
by the current sentimentality of Christendom is surely
no evidence against it. What we have in this denial, as
I have said, is no more than a proof of woman's talent
for a high and sardonic form of comedy and of man's
infinite vanity. "I wooed and won her," says Sganarelle
of his wife. "I made him run," says the hare of the
hound. When the thing is maintained, not as a mere
windy sentimentality, but with some notion of carrying it logically, the result is invariably a display of
paralogy so absurd that it becomes pathetic. Such nonsense one looks for in the works of gyneophile theorists

with no experience of the world, and there is where one finds it. It is almost always wedded to the astounding doctrine that sexual frigidity, already disposed of, is normal in the female, and that the approach of the male is made possible, not by its melting into passion, but by a purely intellectual determination, inwardly revolting, to avoid his ire by pandering to his gross appetites. Thus the thing is stated in a book called "The Sexes in Science and History," by Eliza Burt Gamble, an American lady anthropologist:

The beautiful coloring of male birds and fishes, and the various appendages acquired by males throughout the various orders below man, and which, so far as they themselves are concerned, serve no other useful purpose than to aid them in securing the favours of the females, have by the latter been turned to account in the processes of reproduction. The female made the male beautiful *that she might endure his caresses.*

The italics are mine. From this premiss the learned doctor proceeds to the classical sentimental argument that the males of all species, including man, are little more than chronic seducers, and that their chief energies are devoted to assaulting and breaking down the native reluctance of the æsthetic and anæsthetic females. In her own words: "Regarding males, outside of the instinct for self-preservation, which, by the way is often overshadowed by their great sexual eagerness, no discriminating characters have been acquired and transmitted, *other than those which have been the result of passion,* namely, pugnacity and per-

severance." Again the italics are mine. What we have
here is merely the old, old delusion of masculine
enterprise in amour—the concept of man as a lascivious
monster and of woman as his shrinking victim—in
brief, the Don Juan idea in fresh bib and tucker. In
such bilge lie the springs of many of the most
vexatious delusions of the world, and of some of its
loudest farce no less. It is thus that fatuous old maids
are led to look under their beds for fabulous ravishers,
and to cry out that they have been stabbed with
hypodermic needles in cinema theatres, and to watch
furtively for white slavers in railroad stations. It is
thus, indeed, that the whole white-slave mounte-
bankery has been launched, with its gaudy fictions and
preposterous alarms. And it is thus, more importantly,
that whole regiments of neurotic wives have been
convinced that their children are monuments, not
to a co-operation in which their own share was
innocent and cordial, but to the solitary libidinousness
of their swinish and unconscionable husbands.

Dr. Gamble, of course, is speaking of the lower
fauna in the time of Noah. A literal application of
her theory to man today is enough to bring it to a
reductio ad absurdum. Which sex of *Homo sapiens*
actually does the primping and parading that she
describes? Which runs to "beautiful colouring," sar-
torial, hirsute, facial? Which encases itself in vest-
ments which "serve no other useful purpose than to
aid in securing the favours" of the other? The in-
security of the gifted *savante's* position is at once apparent. The more convincingly she argues that the

primeval mud-hens and she-mackerel had to be an-
æsthetized with spectacular decorations in order to
"endure the caresses" of their beaux, the more she
supports the thesis that men have to be decoyed and
bamboozled into love today. In other words, her argu-
ments turns upon and destroys itself. Carried to its last
implication, it holds that women are all Donna Juanitas,
and that if they put off their millinery and cosmetics,
and abandoned the shameless sexual allurements of their
scanty dress, men could not "endure their caresses."

To be sure, Dr. Gamble by no means draws this
disconcerting conclusion herself. To the contrary, she
clings to the conventional theory that the human
female of today is no more than the plaything of the
concupiscent male, and that she must wait for the
feminist millennium to set her free from his abominable
pawings. But she can reach this notion only by standing her whole structure of reasoning on its head—in
fact, by knocking it over and repudiating it. On the
one hand, she argues that splendour of attire is merely
a bait to overcome the reluctance of the opposite sex,
and on the other hand she argues, at least by fair
inference, that it is not. This grotesque switching of
horses, however, need not detain us. The facts are
too plain to be disposed of by a lady anthropologist's
theorizings. Those facts are supported, in the field of
animal behaviour, by the almost unanimous evidence
of zoologists, including that of Dr. Gamble herself.
They are supported, in the field of human behaviour,
by a body of observation and experience so colossal
that it would be quite out of the question to dispose

of it. Women, as I have shown, have a more delicate æsthetic sense than men; in a world wholly rid of men they would probably still array themselves with vastly more care and thought of beauty than men would ever show in like case. But with the world what it is, it must be obvious that their display of finery—to say nothing of their display of epidermis— has the conscious purpose of attracting the masculine eye. A normal woman, indeed, never so much as buys a pair of shoes or has her teeth plugged without considering, in the back of her mind, the effect upon some unsuspecting candidate for her "reluctant" affections.

19. The Actual Husband

SO FAR AS I can make out, no woman of the sort worth hearing—that is, no woman of intelligence, humour and charm, and hence of success in the duel of sex—has ever publicly denied this; the denial is confined entirely to the absurd sect of female bachelors of arts and to the generality of vain and unobservant men. The former, having failed to attract men by the devices described,

take refuge behind the sour-grapes doctrine that they
have never tried, and the latter, having fallen victims, sooth their egoism by arrogating the whole
agency to themselves, thus giving it a specious appearance of the volitional, and even of the audacious.
The average man is an almost incredible popinjay;
he can think of himself only as at the centre of situations. All the sordid transactions of his life appear
to him, and are depicted in his accounts of them, as
feats, successes, proofs of his acumen. He regards it
as an almost magical exploit to operate a stock-
brokerage shop, or to get elected to public office, or
to swindle his fellow knaves in some degrading com-
mercial enterprise, or to profess some nonsense or
other in a college, or to write so platitudinous a
book as this one. And in the same way he views
it as a great testimony to his prowess at amour to yield
up his liberty, his property and his soul to the first
woman who, in despair of finding better game, turns
her appraising eye upon him. But if you want to hear
a mirthless laugh, just present this masculine theory
to a bridesmaid at a wedding, particularly after alcohol
and crocodile tears have done their disarming work
upon her. That is to say, just hint to her that the
bride harboured no notion of marriage until stormed
into acquiescence by the moonstruck and impetuous
bridegroom.

I have used the phrase, "in despair of finding better
game." What I mean is this: that not one woman in
a hundred ever marries her first choice among mar-
riageable men. That first choice is almost invariably

one who is beyond her talents, for reasons either fortuitous or intrinsic. Let us take, for example, a woman whose relative naiveté makes the process clearly apparent, to wit, a simple shop-girl. Her absolute first choice, perhaps, is not a living man at all, but a supernatural abstraction in a book, say, one of the heroes of Hall Caine, Ethel M. Dell, or Marie Corelli. After him comes a moving-picture actor. Then another moving-picture actor. Then, perhaps, many more—ten or fifteen head. Then a sebaceous young clergyman. Then the junior partner in the firm she works for. Then a couple of department managers. Then a clerk. Then a young man with no definite profession or permanent job—one of the innumerable host which flits from post to post, always restive, always trying something new—perhaps a neighbourhood garage-keeper in the end. Well, the girl begins with the Caine colossus: he vanishes into thin air. She proceeds to the moving picture actors: they are almost as far beyond her. And then to the man of God, the junior partner, the department manager, the clerk: one and all they are carried off by girls of greater attractions and greater skill—girls who can cast gaudier flies. In the end, suddenly terrorized by the first faint shadows of spinsterhood, she turns to the ultimate num-skull—and marries him out of hand.

This, allowing for class modifications, is almost the normal history of a marriage, or, more accurately, of the genesis of a marriage, under Protestant Christianity. Under other rites the business is taken out of the woman's hands, at least partly, and so she is less enterprising in her assembling of candidates and possibilities. But when the whole thing is left to her own heart—*i. e.,* to her head—it is but natural that she should seek as wide a range of choice as the conditions of her life allow, and in a democratic society those conditions put few if any fetters upon her fancy. The servant girl, or factory operative, or even prostitute of today may be the chorus girl or moving picture vampire of tomorrow and the millionaire's wife of next year. In America, especially, men have no settled antipathy to such stooping alliances; in fact, it rather flatters their vanity to play Prince Charming to Cinderella. The result is that every normal American young woman, with the practicality of her sex and the inner confidence that goes therewith, raises her amorous eye as high as it will roll. And the second result is that every American man of presentable exterior and easy means is surrounded by an aura of discreet provocation: he cannot even dictate a letter, or ask for a telephone number without being measured for his wedding coat. On the Continent of Europe, and especially in the Latin countries, where class barriers are more formidable, the situation differs materially, and to the disadvantage of the girl. If she makes an overture, it is an invitation to disaster; her hope of lawful marriage by such means is almost nil. In consequence, the prudent and decent girl avoids such overtures, and they must be made by third parties or by the man himself. This is the explanation of the fact that a Frenchman, say, is habitually enterprising in amour, and hence bold and often offensive, whereas an American is what is called chivalrous. The American is chivalrous for the simple reason that the initiative is not in his hands. His chivalry is really a sort of coquetry.

20. *The Unattainable Ideal*

BUT HERE I rather depart from the point, which is this: that the average woman is not strategically capable of bringing down the most tempting game within her purview, and must thus content herself with a second, third, or *n*th choice. The only women who get their first choices are those who run in almost miraculous luck and those too stupid to formulate an ideal—two very small classes, it must be obvious. A few women, true enough, are so pertinacious that they prefer defeat to compromise. That is to say, they prefer to put off marriage indefinitely rather than to marry beneath the highest leap of their fancy. But such women may be quickly dismissed as abnormal, and perhaps as downright diseased in mind; the average woman is well aware that marriage is far better for her than celibacy, even when it falls a good deal short of her primary hopes, and she is also well aware that the differences between man and man, once mere money is put aside, are so slight as to be practically almost negligible. Thus the average woman is under none of the common masculine illusions about elective affinities, soul mates, love at first sight, and such phantasms. She is quite ready to fall in love, as the phrase is, with any man who is plainly eligible, and she usually knows a good many more such men than one. Her primary demand in marriage is not for the agonies of romance, but for comfort and security; she is thus easier satisfied than a man, and oftener happy. One frequently hears of remarried widowers who continue to moon about their dead first wives, but for a remarried widow to show any such sentimentality would be a nine days' wonder. Once replaced, a dead husband is expunged from the minutes. And so is a dead love.

One of the results of all this is a subtle reinforcement of the contempt with which women normally regard their husbands—a contempt grounded, as I have shown, upon a sense of intellectual superiority. To this primary sense of superiority is now added the disparagement of a concrete comparison, and over all is an ineradicable resentment of the fact that such a comparison has been necessary. In other words, the typical husband is a second-rater, and no one is better aware of it than his wife. He is, taking averages, one who has been loved, as the saying goes, by but one woman, and then only as a second, third or nth choice. If any other woman had ever loved him, as the idiom has it, she would have married him, and so made him ineligible for his present happiness. But the average bachelor is a man who has been loved, so to speak, by many women, and is the lost first choice of at least some of them. He represents the unattainable, and hence the admirable; the husband is the attained and disdained.

Here we have a sufficient explanation of the general superiority of bachelors, so often noted by students of mankind—a superiority so marked that it is difficult, in all history, to find six first-rate philosophers who were married men. The bachelor's very capacity to avoid marriage is no more than a proof of his relative freedom from the ordinary sentimentalism of his sex—in other words, of his greater approximation to the clearheadedness of the enemy sex. He is able to defeat the enterprise of women because he brings to the business an equipment almost comparable to their own. Herbert Spencer, until he was fifty, was ferociously harassed by women of all sorts. Among others, George Eliot tried very desperately to marry him. But after he had made it plain, over a long series of years, that he was prepared to resist marriage to the full extent of his military and naval power, the girls dropped off one by one, and so his last decades were full of peace and he got a great deal of very important work done.

T IS, OF COURSE, not well for the world that the highest sort of men are thus selected out, as the biologists say, and that their superiority dies with them, whereas the ignoble tricks and sentimentalities of lesser men are infinitely propagated. Despite a popular delusion that the sons of great men are always dolts, the fact is that intellectual superiority is inheritable quite as easily as bodily strength; and that fact has been established beyond cavil by the laborious inquiries of Galton, Pearson and the other anthropometricians of the English school. If such men as Spinoza, Kant, Schopenhauer, Spencer, and Nietzsche had married and begotten sons, those sons, it is probable, would have contributed as much to philosophy as the sons and grandsons of Veit Bach contributed to music, or those of Erasmus Darwin to biology, or those of Henry Adams to politics, or those of Hamilcar Barca to the art of war. I have said that Herbert Spencer's escape from marriage facilitated his life-work, and so served the immediate good of English philosophy, but in the long run it will work a detriment, for he left no sons to carry on his labours, and the remaining Englishmen of his time were unable to supply the lack. His celibacy, indeed, made English philosophy co-extensive with his life; since his death the whole body of metaphysical speculation produced in England has been of little more practical value to the world than a drove of hogs. In precisely the same way the celibacy of Schopenhauer, Kant and Nietzsche has reduced German philosophy to feebleness.

Even setting aside this direct influence of heredity, there is the equally potent influence of example and tuition. It is a gigantic advantage to live on intimate terms with a first-rate man, and have his care. Hamilcar not only gave the Carthagenians a great general in his actual son; he also gave them a great general in his son-in-law, trained in his camp. But the tendency of the first-rate man to remain a bachelor is very strong, and Sidney Lee once showed that, of all the great writers of England since the Renaissance, more than half were either celibates or lived apart from their wives. Even the married ones revealed the tendency plainly. For example, consider Shakespeare. He was forced into marriage while still a minor by the brothers of Ann Hathaway, who was several years his senior, and had debauched him and gave out that she was *enceinte* by him. He escaped from her abhorrent embraces as quickly as possible, and thereafter kept as far away from her as he could. His very distaste for marriage, indeed, was the cause of his residence in London, and hence, in all probability, of the labours which made him immortal.

In different parts of the world various expedients have been resorted to to overcome this reluctance to marriage among the better sort of men. Christianity, in general, combats it on the ground that it is offensive to God—though at the same time leaning toward an enforced celibacy among its own agents. The discrepancy is fatal to the position. On the one hand, it is impossible to believe that the same God who permitted His own son to die a bachelor regards celibacy as an actual sin, and on the other hand, it is obvious that the average cleric would be damaged but little, and probably improved appreciably, by having a wife to think for him, and to force him to virtue and industry, and to aid him otherwise in his sordid profession. Where religious superstitions have died out the institution of the *dot* prevails—an idea borrowed by Christians from the Jews. The *dot* is simply a bribe designed to overcome the disinclination of the male. It involves a frank recognition of the fact that he loses by marriage, and it seeks to make up for that loss by a money payment. Its obvious effect is to give young women a wider and better choice of husbands. A relatively superior man, otherwise quite out of reach, may be brought into camp by the assurance of economic ease, and what is more, he may be kept in order after he has been taken by the consciousness of his gain. Among hardheaded and highly practical peoples, such as the Jews and the French, the *dot* flourishes, and its effect is to promote intellectual suppleness in the race, for the average child is thus not inevitably the offspring of a woman and a noodle, as with us, but may be the offspring of a woman and a man of reasonable intelligence. But even in France, the very highest class of men tend to evade marriage; they resist money almost as unanimously as their Anglo-Saxon brethren resist sentimentality.

In America the *dot* is almost unknown, partly because money-getting is easier to men than in Europe and is regarded as less degrading, and partly because American men are more naïve than Frenchmen and are thus readily intrigued without actual bribery. But the best of them nevertheless lean to celibacy, and plans for overcoming their habit are frequently proposed and discussed. One such plan involves a heavy tax on bachelors. The defect in it lies in the fact that the average bachelor, for obvious reasons, is relatively well to do, and would pay the tax rather than marry. Moreover, the payment of it would help to salve his conscience, which is now often made restive, I believe, by a maudlin feeling that he is shirking his duty to the race, and so he would be confirmed and supported in his determination to avoid the altar. Still further, he would escape the social odium which now attaches to his celibacy, for whatever a man pays for is regarded as his right. As things stand, that odium is of definite potency, and undoubtedly has its influence upon a certain number of men in the lower ranks of bachelors. They stand, so to speak, in the twilight zone of bachelorhood, with one leg furtively over the altar rail; it needs only an extra pull to bring them to the sacrifice. But if they could compound for their immunity by a cash indemnity it is highly probable that they would take on new resolution, and in the end they would convert what remained of their present disrepute into a source of egoistic satisfaction, as is done, indeed, by a great many bachelors even today. These last immoralists are privy to the elements which enter into that disrepute: the ire of women whose devices they have resisted and the envy of men who have succumbed.

22. Compulsory Marriage

MYSELF once proposed an alternative scheme, to wit, the prohibition of sentimental marriages by law, and the substitution of match-making by the common hangman. This plan, as revolutionary as it may seem, would have several plain advantages. For one thing, it would purge the serious business of marriage of the romantic fol-de-rol that now corrupts it, and so make for the peace and happiness of the race. For another thing, it would work against the process which now selects out, as I have said, those men who are most fit, and so throws the chief burden of paternity upon the inferior, to the damage of posterity. The hangman, if he made his selections arbitrarily, would try to give his office permanence and dignity by choosing men whose marriage would meet with public approbation, *i. e.,* men obviously of sound stock and talents, *i. e.,* the sort of men who now habitually escape. And if he made his selection by the hazard of the die, or by drawing numbers out of a hat, or by any other such method of pure chance, that pure chance would fall indiscriminately upon all orders of men, and the upper orders would thus lose their present comparative immunity. True enough, a good many men would endeavour to influence him privately to their own advantage, and it is probable that he would occasionally succumb, but it must be plain that the men most likely to prevail in that enterprise would not be philosophers, but politicians, and so there would be some benefit to the race even here. Posterity surely suffers no very heavy loss when a Congressman, a member of the House of Lords or even an ambassador or Prime Minister dies childless, but when a Herbert Spencer goes to the grave without leaving sons behind him there is a detriment to all the generations of the future.

I did not offer the plan, of course, as a contribution to practical politics, but merely as a sort of hypothesis, to help clarify the problem. Many other theoretical advantages appear in it, but its execution is made impossible, not only by inherent defects, but also by a general disinclination to abandon the present system, which at least offers certain attractions to concrete men and women, despite its unfavourable effects upon the unborn. Women would oppose the substitution of chance or arbitrary fiat for the existing struggle for the plain reason that every woman is convinced, and no doubt rightly, that her own judgment is superior to that of either the common hangman or the gods, and that her own enterprise is more favourable to her opportunities. And men would oppose it because it would restrict their liberty. This liberty, of course, is largely imaginary. In its common manifestation, it is no more, at bottom, than the privilege of being bamboozled and made a mock of by the first woman who ventures to essay the business. But none the less it is quite as precious to men as any other of the ghosts that their vanity conjures up for their enchantment. They cherish the notion that unconditioned volition enters into the matter, and that under volition there is not only a high degree of sagacity but also a touch of the daring and the devilish. A man is often almost as much pleased and flattered by his own marriage as he would be by the achievement of what is currently called a seduction. In the one case, as in the other, his emotion is one of triumph. The substitution of pure chance would take away that soothing unction.

The present system, to be sure, also involves chance. Every man realizes it, and even the most bombastic bachelor has moments in which he humbly whispers: "There, but for the grace of God, go I." But that chance has a sugar-coating; it is swathed in egoistic illusion; it shows less stark and intolerable chanciness, so to speak, than the bald hazard of the die. Thus men prefer it, and shrink from the other. In the same way, I have no doubt, the majority of foxes would object to choosing lots to determine the victim of a projected fox-hunt. They prefer to take their chances with the dogs.

23. *Extra-Legal Devices*

IT IS, OF COURSE, a rhetorical exaggeration to say that *all* first-class men escape marriage, and even more of an exaggeration to say that their high qualities go wholly untransmitted to posterity. On the one hand it must be obvious that an appreciable number of them, perhaps by reason of their very detachment and preoccupation, are intrigued into the holy estate, and that not a few of them enter it deliberately, convinced that it is the safest form of liaison possible under Christianity. And on the other hand one must not forget the biological fact that it is quite feasible to achieve offspring without the imprimatur of Church and State. The thing, indeed, is so commonplace that I need not risk a scandal by uncovering it in detail. What I allude to, I need not add, is not that form of irregularity which curses innocent children with the stigma of illegitimacy, but that more refined and thoughtful form which safeguards their social dignity while protecting them against inheritance from their legal fathers. English philosophy, as I have shown, suffers by the fact that Herbert Spencer was too busy to permit himself any such romantic altruism —just as American literature gains enormously by the fact that Walt Whitman adventured, leaving seven sons behind him, three of whom are now well-known American poets and in the forefront of the New Poetry movement.

The extent of this correction of a salient evil of monogamy is very considerable; its operations explain the private disrepute of perhaps a majority of first-rate men; its advantages have been set forth in George Moore's "Euphorion in Texas," though in a clumsy and sentimental way. What is behind it is the profound race-sense of women—the instinct which makes them regard the unborn in their every act—perhaps, too, the fact that the interests of the unborn are here identical, as in other situations, with their own egoistic aspirations. As a popular philosopher has shrewdly observed, the objections to polygamy do not come from women, for the average woman is sensible enough to prefer half or a quarter or even a tenth of a first-rate man to the whole devotion of a third-rate man. Considerations of much the same sort also justify polyandry—if not morally, then at least biologically. The average woman, as I have shown, must inevitably view her actual husband with a certain disdain; he is anything but her ideal. In consequence, she cannot help feeling that her children are cruelly handicapped by the fact that he is their father, nor can she help feeling guilty about it; for she knows that he is their father only by reason of her own initiative in the proceedings anterior to her marriage. If, now, an opportunity presents itself to remove that handicap from at least some of them, and at the same time to realize her ideal and satisfy her vanity—if such a chance offers it is no wonder that she occasionally embraces it.

Here we have an explanation of many lamentable and otherwise inexplicable violations of domestic integrity. The woman in the case is commonly dismissed as vicious, but that is no more than a new example of the common human tendency to attach the concept of viciousness to whatever is natural, and intelligent, and above the comprehension of politicians, theologians and green-grocers.

24. Intermezzo on Monogamy

THE PREVALENCE of monogamy in Christendom is commonly ascribed to ethical motives. This is quite as absurd as ascribing wars to ethical motives—which is, of course, frequently done. The simple truth is that ethical motives are no more than deductions from experience, and that they are quickly abandoned whenever experience turns against them. In the present case experience is still overwhelming on the side of monogamy; civilized men are in favour of it because they find that it works. And why does it work? Because it is the most effective of all available antidotes to the alarms and terrors of passion. Monogamy, in brief, kills passion—and passion is the most dangerous of all the surviving enemies to what we call civilization, which is based upon order, decorum, restraint, formality, industry, regimentation. The civilized man—the ideal civilized man—is simply one who never sacrifices the common security to his private passions. He reaches perfection when he even ceases to love passionately—when he reduces the most profound of all his instinctive experiences from the level of an ecstasy to the level of a mere device for replenishing the armies and workshops of the world, keeping clothes in repair, reducing the infant death-rate, providing enough tenants for every landlord, and making it possible for the *Polizei* to know where every citizen is at any hour of the day or night. Monogamy accomplishes this, not by producing satiety, but by destroying appetite. It makes passion formal and uninspiring, and so gradually kills it.

The advocates of monogamy, deceived by its moral overtones, fail to get all the advantage out of it that is in it. Consider, for example, the important moral business of safeguarding the virtue of the unmarried— that is, of the still passionate. The present plan in dealing, say, with a young man of twenty, is to surround him with scare-crows and prohibitions—to try to convince him logically that passion is dangerous. This is both supererogation and imbecility—supererogation because he already knows that it is dangerous, and imbecility because it is quite impossible to kill a passion by arguing against it. The way to kill it is to give it

rein under unfavourable and dispiriting conditions—
to bring it down, by slow stages, to the estate of an
absurdity and a horror. How much more, then, could
be accomplished if the wild young man were forbidden
polygamy, before marriage, but permitted monogamy!
The prohibition in this case would be relatively easy to
enforce, instead of impossible, as in the other. Curiosity
would be satisfied; nature would get out of her cage;
even romance would get an inning. Ninety-nine young
men out of a hundred would submit, if only because
it would be much easier to submit than to resist.

And the result? Obviously, it would be laudable—
that is, accepting current definitions of the laudable.
The product, after six months, would be a well-regi-
mented and disillusioned young man, as devoid of
disquieting and demoralizing passion as an ancient
of eighty—in brief, the ideal citizen of Christendom.
The present plan surely fails to produce a satisfactory
crop of such ideal citizens. On the one hand its impossible prohibitions cause a multitude of lamentable revolts, often ending in a silly sort of running amok.
On the other hand they fill the Y. M. C. A.'s with
scared poltroons full of indescribably disgusting
Freudian suppressions. Neither group supplies many
ideal citizens. Neither promotes the sort of public
morality that is aimed at.

25. Late Marriages

HE MARRIAGE of a first-rate man, when it takes place at all, commonly takes place relatively late. He may succumb in the end, but he is almost always able to postpone the disaster a good deal longer than the average poor clodpate, or normal man. If he actually marries early, it is nearly always proof that some intolerable external pressure has been applied to him, as in Shakespeare's case, or that his mental sensitiveness approaches downright insanity, as in Shelley's. This fact, curiously enough, has escaped the observation of an otherwise extremely astute observer, namely Havelock Ellis. In his study of British genius he notes the fact that most men of unusual capacities are the sons of relatively old fathers, but instead of exhibiting the true cause thereof, he ascribes it to a mysterious quality whereby a man already in decline is capable of begetting better offspring than one in full vigour. This is a palpable absurdity, not only because it goes counter to facts long established by animal breeders, but also because it tacitly assumes that talent, and hence the capacity for transmitting it, is an acquired character, and that this character may be transmitted. Nothing could be more unsound. Talent is not an acquired character, but a congenital character, and the man who is born with it has it in early life quite as well as in later life, though its manifestation may have to wait. James Mill was yet a young man when his son, John Stuart Mill, was born, and not one of his principle books had been written. But though the "Elements of Political Economy" and the "Analysis of the Human Mind" were thus but vaguely formulated in his mind, if they were actually so much as formulated at all, and it was fifteen years before he wrote them, he was still quite able to transmit the capacity to write them to his son, and that capacity showed itself, years afterward, in the latter's "Principles of Political Economy" and "Essay on Liberty."

But Ellis' faulty inference is still based upon a sound observation, to wit, that the sort of man capable of transmitting high talents to a son is ordinarily a man who does not have a son at all, at least in wedlock, until he has advanced into middle life. The reasons which impel him to yield even then are somewhat obscure, but two or three of them, perhaps, may be vaguely discerned. One lies in the fact that every man, whether of the first class or of any other class, tends to decline in mental agility as he grows older, though in the actual range and profundity of his intelligence he may keep on improving until he collapses into senility. Obviously, it is mere agility of mind, and not profundity, that is of most value and effect in so tricky and deceptive a combat as the duel of sex. The aging man, with his agility gradually withering, is thus confronted by women in whom it still luxuriates as a function of their relative youth. Not only do women of his own age aspire to ensnare him, but also women of all ages back to adolescence. Hence his average or typical opponent tends to be progressively younger and younger than he is, and in the end the mere advantage of her youth may be sufficient to tip over his tottering defences. This, I take it, is why oldish men are so often intrigued by girls in their teens. It is not that age calls maudlinly to youth, as the poets would have it; it is that age is no match for youth, especially when age is male and youth is female. The case of the late Henrik Ibsen was typical. At forty Ibsen was a sedate family man, and it is doubtful that he ever so much as glanced at a woman; all his thoughts were upon the composition of "The League of Youth," his first social drama. At fifty he was almost as preoccupied; "A Doll's House" was then hatching. But at sixty, with his best work all done and his decline begun, he succumbed preposterously to a flirtatious damsel of eighteen, and thereafter, until actual insanity released him, he mooned like a provincial actor in a sentimental melodrama. Had it not been, indeed, for the fact that he was already married, and to a very sensible wife, he would have run off with this flapper, and so made himself publicly ridiculous.

Another reason for the relatively late marriages of superior men is found, perhaps, in the fact that, as a man grows older, the disabilities he suffers by marriage tend to diminish and the advantages to increase. At thirty a man is terrified by the inhibitions of monogamy and has little taste for the so-called comforts of a home; at sixty he is beyond amorous adventure and is in need of creature ease and security. What he

is oftenest conscious of, in these later years, is his physical decay; he sees himself as in imminent danger of
falling into neglect and helplessness. He is thus confronted by a choice between getting a wife or hiring a
nurse, and he commonly chooses the wife as the less
expensive and exacting. The nurse, indeed, would probably try to marry him anyhow; if he employs her in
place of a wife he commonly ends by finding himself
married and minus a nurse, to his confusion and discomfiture, and to the far greater discomfiture of his
heirs and assigns. This process is so obvious and so
commonplace that I apologize formally for rehearsing
it. What it indicates is simply this: that a man's instinctive aversion to marriage is grounded upon a sense of
social and economic self-sufficiency, and that it descends
into a mere theory when this self-sufficiency disappears.
After all, nature is on the side of mating, and hence
on the side of marriage, and vanity is a powerful ally of
nature. If men, at the normal mating age, had half as
much to gain by marriage as women gain, then all
men would be as ardently in favour of it as women are.

26. Disparate Unions

THIS BRINGS us to a fact
frequently noted by students of the subject: that first-
rate men, when they marry at all, tend to marry notice-

ably inferior wives. The causes of the phenomenon, so often discussed and so seldom illuminated, should be plain by now. The first-rate man, by postponing marriage as long as possible, often approaches it in the end with his faculties crippled by senility, and is thus open to the advances of women whose attractions are wholly meretricious, *e. g.,* empty flappers, scheming widows, and trained nurses with a highly developed professional technic of sympathy. If he marries at all, indeed, he must commonly marry badly, for women of genuine merit are no longer interested in him; what was once a lodestar is now no more than a smoking smudge. It is this circumstance that accounts for the low calibre of a good many first-rate men's sons, and gives a certain support to the common notion that they are always third-raters. Those sons inherit from their mothers as well as from their fathers, and the bad strain is often sufficient to obscure and nullify the good strain. Mediocrity, as every Mendelian knows, is a dominant character, and extraordinary ability is a recessive character. In a marriage between an able man and a commonplace woman, the chances that any given child will resemble the mother are, roughly speaking, three to one.

The fact suggests the thought that nature is secretly against the superman, and seeks to prevent his birth. We have, indeed, no ground for assuming that the continued progress visualized by man is in actual accord with the great flow of the elemental forces. Devolution is quite as natural as evolution, and may be just as pleasing, or even a good deal more pleasing, to God. If the average man is made in God's image, then a

man such as Beethoven or Aristotle is plainly superior
to God, and so God may be jealous of him, and eager
to see his superiority perish with his bodily frame. All
animal breeders know how difficult it is to maintain a
fine strain. The universe seems to be in a conspiracy
to encourage the endless reproduction of peasants and
Socialists, but a subtle and mysterious opposition stands
eternally against the reproduction of philosophers.

Per corollary, it is notorious that women of merit
frequently marry second-rate men, and bear them children, thus aiding in the war upon progress. One is
often astonished to discover that the wife of some sordid
and prosaic manufacturer or banker or professional
man is a woman of quick intelligence and genuine
charm, with intellectual interests so far above his comprehension that he is scarcely so much as aware of them.
Again, there are the leading feminists, women artists
and other such captains of the sex; their husbands are
almost always inferior men, and sometimes downright
fools. But not paupers! Not incompetents in a man's
world! Not bad husbands! What we here encounter,
of course, is no more than a fresh proof of the sagacity
of women. The first-rate woman is a realist. She sees
clearly that, in a world dominated by second-rate men,
the special capacities of the second-rate man are
esteemed above all other capacities and given the highest rewards, and she endeavours to get her share of
those rewards by marrying a second-rate man at the
top of his class. The first-rate man is an admirable creature; his qualities are appreciated by every intelligent
woman; as I have just said, it may be reasonably argued
that he is actually superior to God. But his attractions,

after a certain point, do not run in proportion to his deserts; beyond that he ceases to be a good husband. Hence the pursuit of him is chiefly maintained, not by women who are his peers, but by women who are his inferiors.

Here we unearth another factor: the fascination of what is strange, the charm of the unlike, *héliogabalisme*. As Shakespeare has put it, there must be some mystery in love—and there can be no mystery between intellectual equals. I daresay that many a woman marries an inferior man, not primarily because he is a good provider (though it is impossible to imagine her overlooking this), but because his very inferiority interests her, and makes her want to remedy it and mother him. Egoism is in the impulse: it is pleasant to have a feeling of superiority, and to be assured that it can be maintained. If now, that feeling be mingled with sexual curiosity and economic self-interest, it obviously supplies sufficient motivation to account for so natural and banal a thing as a marriage. Perhaps the greatest of all these factors is the mere disparity, the naked strangeness. A woman could not love a man, as the phrase is, who wore skirts and pencilled his eyebrows, and by the same token she would probably find it difficult to love a man who matched perfectly her own sharpness of mind. What she most esteems in marriage, on the psychic plane, is the chance it offers for the exercise of that caressing irony which I have already described. She likes to observe that her man is a fool—dear, perhaps, but none the less damned. Her so-called love for him, even at its highest, is always somewhat pitying and patronizing.

ONOGAMOUS marriage, by its very conditions, tends to break down this strangeness. It forces the two contracting parties into an intimacy that is too persistent and unmitigated; they are in contact at too many points, and too steadily. By and by all the mystery of the relation is gone, and they stand in the unsexed position of brother and sister. Thus that "maximum of temptation" of which Shaw speaks has within itself the seeds of its own decay. A husband begins by kissing a pretty girl, his wife; it is pleasant to have her so handy and so willing. He ends by making machiavellian efforts to avoid kissing the every day sharer of his meals, books, bath towels, pocketbook, relatives, ambitions, secrets, malaises and business: a proceeding about as romantic as having his boots blacked. The thing is too horribly dismal for words. Not all the native sentimentalism of man can overcome the distaste and boredom that get into it. Not all the histrionic capacity of woman can attach any appearance of gusto and spontaneity to it.

An estimable lady psychologist of the American
Republic, Mrs. Marion Cox, in a somewhat florid
book entitled "Ventures into Worlds," has a sagacious
essay upon this subject. She calls the essay "Our In-
cestuous Marriage," and argues accurately that, once
the adventurous descends to the habitual, it takes on an
offensive and degrading character. The intimate approach, to give genuine joy, must be a concession, a
feat of persuasion, a victory; once it loses that character
it loses everything. Such a destructive conversion is
effected by the average monogamous marriage. It
breaks down all mystery and reserve, for how can
mystery and reserve survive the use of the same hot
water bag and a joint concern about butter and egg
bills? What remains, at least on the husband's side,
is esteem—the feeling one has for an amiable aunt.
And confidence—the emotion evoked by a lawyer, a
dentist or a fortune-teller. And habit—the thing which
makes it possible to eat the same breakfast every day,
and to wind up one's watch regularly, and to earn a
living.

Mrs. Cox, if I remember her dissertation correctly,
proposes to prevent this stodgy dephlogistication of
marriage by interrupting its course—that is, by separating the parties now and then, so that neither will become too familiar and commonplace to the other. By
this means, she argues, curiosity will be periodically
revived, and there will be a chance for personality to
expand *a cappella,* and so each reunion will have in
it something of the surprise, the adventure and the
virtuous satanry of the honeymoon. The husband will

not come back to precisely the same wife that he parted from, and the wife will not welcome precisely the same husband. Even supposing them to have gone on substantially as if together, they will have gone on out of sight and hearing of each other. Thus each will find the other, to some extent at least, a stranger, and hence a bit challenging, and hence a bit charming. The scheme has merit. More, it has been tried often, and with success. It is, indeed, a familiar observation that the happiest couples are those who are occasionally separated, and the fact has been embalmed in the trite maxim that absence makes the heart grow fonder. Perhaps not actually fonder, but at any rate more tolerant, more curious, more eager. Two difficulties, however, stand in the way of the widespread adoption of the remedy. One lies in its costliness: the average couple cannot afford a double establishment, even temporarily. The other lies in the fact that it inevitably arouses the envy and ill-nature of those who cannot adopt it, and so causes a gabbling of scandal. The world invariably suspects the worst. Let man and wife separate to save their happiness from suffocation in the kitchen, the dining room and the connubial chamber, and it will immediately conclude that the corpse is already laid out in the drawing-room.

HIS BOREDOM of mar-
riage, however, is not nearly so dangerous a menace to
the institution as Mrs. Cox, with evangelistic enthusiasm, permits herself to think it is. It bears most harshly
upon the wife, who is almost always the more intelligent of the pair; in the case of the husband its pains
are usually lightened by that sentimentality with which
men dilute the disagreeable, particularly in marriage.
Moreover, the average male gets his living by such
depressing devices that boredom becomes a sort of natural state to him. A man who spends six or eight hours
a day acting as teller in a bank, or sitting upon the
bench of a court, or looking to the inexpressibly trivial
details of some process of manufacturing, or writing
imbecile articles for a newspaper, or managing a tram-
way, or administering ineffective medicines to stupid
and uninteresting patients—a man so engaged during
all his hours of labour, which means a normal, typical
man, is surely not one to be oppressed unduly by the
dull round of domesticity. His wife may bore him
hopelessly as mistress, just as any other mistress inevitably bores a man (though surely not so quickly
and so painfully as a lover bores a woman), but she

is not apt to bore him so badly in her other capacities.
What he commonly complains about in her, in truth,
is not that she tires him by her monotony, but that
she tires him by her variety—not that she is too
static, but that she is too dynamic. He is weary when
he gets home, and asks only the dull peace of a hog in a
comfortable sty. This peace is broken by the greater
restlessness of his wife, the fruit of her greater intellectual resilience and curiosity.

Of far more potency as a cause of connubial discord
is the general inefficiency of a woman at the business
of what is called keeping house—a business founded
upon a complex of trivial technicalities. As I have
argued at length, women are congenitally less fitted
for mastering these technicalities than men; the enterprise always costs them more effort, and they are
never able to reinforce mere diligent application with
that obtuse enthusiasm which men commonly bring
to their tawdry and childish concerns. But in addition
to their natural incapacity, there is a reluctance based
upon a deficiency in incentive, and that deficiency in
incentive is due to the maudlin sentimentality with
which men regard marriage. In this sentimentality lie
the germs of most of the evils which beset the institution in Christendom, and particularly in the United
States, where sentiment is always carried to inordinate
lengths. Having abandoned the mediaeval concept of
woman as temptress, the men of the Nordic race have
revived the correlative mediaeval concept of woman
as angel, and to bolster up that character they have
created for her a vast and growing mass of immunities,

culminating of late years in the astounding doctrine that, under the contract of marriage, all the duties lie upon the man and all the privileges appertain to the woman. In part this doctrine has been established by the intellectual enterprise and audacity of woman. Bit by bit, playing upon masculine stupidity, sentimentality and lack of strategical sense, they have formulated it, developed it, and entrenched it in custom and law. But in other part it is the plain product of the donkeyish vanity which makes almost every man view the practical incapacity of his wife as, in some vague way, a tribute to his own high mightiness and consideration. Whatever his revolt against her immediate indolence and efficiency, his ideal is nearly always a situation in which she will figure as a magnificent drone, a sort of empress without portfolio, entirely discharged from every unpleasant labour and responsibility.

29. Marriage and the Law

THIS WAS NOT always the case. No more than a century ago, even by American law, the most sentimental in the world, the husband was the head of the family firm, lordly and autonomous. He had authority over the purse-strings, over the children, and even over his wife. He could enforce his mandates by appropriate punishment, including the corporal. His sovereignty and dignity were carefully guarded by legislation, the product of thousands of years of experience and ratiocination. He was safe-guarded in his self-respect by the most elaborate and efficient devices, and they had the support of public opinion.

Consider, now, the changes that a few short years have wrought. Today, by the laws of most American states—laws proposed, in most cases, by maudlin and often notoriously extravagant agitators, and passed by sentimental orgy—all of the old rights of the husband have been converted into obligations. He no longer has any control over his wife's property; she may devote its income to the family or she may squander that income upon idle follies, and he can do nothing. She has equal authority in regulating and disposing of the children, and, in the case of infants, more than he. There is no law compelling her to do her share of the family labour: she may spend her whole time in cinema theatres or gadding about the shops as she will. She cannot be forced to perpetuate the family name if she does not want to. She cannot be attacked with mascu-line weapons, *e. g.,* fists and firearms, when she makes an assault with feminine weapons, *e. g.,* snuffling, in-vective and sabotage. Finally, no lawful penalty can be visited upon her if she fails absolutely, either deliberately or through mere incapacity, to keep the family habitat clean, the children in order, and the victuals eatable.

Now view the situation of the husband. The in-stant he submits to marriage, his wife obtains a large

and inalienable share in his property, including all he
may acquire in future; in most American states the
minimum is one-third, and, failing children, one-half.
He cannot dispose of his real estate without her con-
sent; he cannot even deprive her of it by will. She
may bring up his children carelessly and idiotically,
cursing them with abominable manners and poisoning
their nascent minds against him, and he has no re-
dress. She may neglect her home, gossip and lounge
about all day, put impossible food upon his table, steal
his small change, pry into his private papers, hand
over his home to the *Periplaneta americana,* accuse
him falsely of preposterous adulteries, affront his
friends, and lie about him to the neighbours—and he
can do nothing. She may compromise his honour by
indecent dressing, write letters to moving-picture
actors, and expose him to ridicule by going into politics
—and he is helpless.

Let him undertake the slightest rebellion, over and
beyond mere rhetorical protest, and the whole force
of the state comes down upon him. If he corrects her
with the bastinado or locks her up, he is good for
six months in jail. If he cuts off her revenues, he is
incarcerated until he makes them good. And if he
seeks surcease in flight, taking the children with him,
he is pursued by the *gendarmerie,* brought back to
his duties, and depicted in the public press as a
scoundrelly kidnapper, fit only for the knout. In brief,
she is under no legal necessity whatsoever to carry out
her part of the compact at the altar of God, whereas
he faces instant disgrace and punishment for the

slightest failure to observe its last letter. For a few grave crimes of commission, true enough, she may be proceeded against. Open adultery is a recreation that is denied to her. She cannot poison her husband. She must not assault him with edged tools, or leave him altogether, or strip off her few remaining garments and go naked. But for the vastly more various and numerous crimes of omission—and in sum they are more exasperating and intolerable than even overt felony—she cannot be brought to book at all.

The scene I depict is American, but it will soon extend its horrors to all Protestant countries. The newly-enfranchised women of every one of them cherish long programs of what they call social improvement, and practically the whole of that improvement is based upon devices for augmenting their own relative autonomy and power. The English wife of tradition, so thoroughly a *femme covert,* is being displaced by a gadabout, truculent, irresponsible creature, full of strange new ideas about her rights, and strongly disinclined to submit to her husband's authority, or to devote herself honestly to the upkeep of his house, or to bear him a biological sufficiency of heirs. And the German *Hausfrau,* once so innocently consecrated to *Kirche, Küche und Kinder,* is going the same way.

30. The Emancipated Housewife

WHAT HAS GONE on in the United States during the past two generations is full of lessons and warnings for the rest of the world. The American housewife of an earlier day was famous for her unremitting diligence. She not only cooked, washed and ironed; she also made shift to master such more complex arts as spinning, baking and brewing. Her expertness, perhaps, never reached a high level, but at all events she made a gallant effort. But that was long, long ago, before the new enlightenment rescued her. Today, in her average incarnation, she is not only incompetent (a lack, as I have argued, rather beyond her control); she is also filled with the notion that a conscientious discharge of her few remaining duties is, in some vague way, discreditable and degrading. To call her a good cook, I daresay, was never anything but flattery; the early American cuisine was probably a fearful thing, indeed. But today the flattery turns into a sort of libel, and she resents it, or, at all events, does not welcome it. I used to know an American literary man, educated on the Continent, who married a woman because she had exceptional gifts in this department. Years later, at one of her dinners, a friend of her husband's tried to please her by mentioning the fact, to which he had always been privy. But instead of being complimented, as a man might have been if told that his wife had married him because he was a good lawyer, or surgeon, or blacksmith, this unusual housekeeper, suffering a renaissance of usualness, denounced the guest as a liar, ordered him out of the house, and threatened to leave her husband.

This disdain of offices that, after all, are necessary, and might as well be faced with some show of cheerfulness, takes on the character of a definite cult in the United States, and the stray woman who attends to them faithfully is laughed at as a drudge and a fool, just as she is apt to be dismissed as a "brood sow" (I quote literally, craving absolution for the phrase: a jury of men during the late war, on very thin patriotic grounds, jailed the author of it) if she favours her lord with viable issue. One result is the notorious villainousness of American cookery—a villainousness so painful to a cultured uvula that a French hack-driver, if his wife set its masterpieces before him, would brain her with his linoleum hat. To encounter a decent meal in an American home of the middle class, simple, sensibly chosen and competently cooked, becomes almost as startling as to meet a Y.M.C.A. secretary in a bordello, and a good deal rarer. Such a thing, in most of the large cities of the Republic, scarcely has any existence. If the average American husband wants a sound dinner he must go to a restaurant to get it, just as if he wants to refresh himself with the society of charming and well-behaved children, he has to go to an orphan asylum. Only the immigrant can take his ease and invite his soul within his own house.

IV
WOMAN
SUFFRAGE

31. The Crowning Victory

I T IS MY sincere hope that nothing I have here exhibited will be mistaken by the nobility and gentry for moral indignation. No such feeling, in truth, is in my heart. Moral judgments, as old Friedrich used to say, are foreign to my nature. Setting aside the vast herd which shows no definable character at all, it seems to me that the minority distinguished by what is commonly regarded as an excess of sin is very much more admirable than the minority distinguished by an excess of virtue. My experience of the world has taught me that the average wine-bibber is a far better fellow than the average prohibitionist, and that the average rogue is better company than the average poor drudge, and that the worst white-slave trader of my acquaintance is a decenter man than the best vice crusader. In the same way I am convinced that the average woman, whatever her deficiencies, is greatly superior to the average man. The very ease with which she defies and swindles him in several capital situations of life is the clearest of proofs of her general superiority. She did not obtain her present high immunities as a gift from the gods, but only after a long and often bitter fight, and in that fight she exhibited forensic and tactical talents of a truly admirable order. There was no weakness of man that she did not penetrate and take advantage of. There was no trick that she did not put to effective use. There was no device so bold and inordinate that it daunted her.

The latest and greatest fruit of this feminine talent for combat is the extension of the suffrage, now universal in the Protestant countries, and even advancing in those of the Greek and Latin rites. This fruit was garnered, not by an attack *en masse,* but by a mere foray. I believe that the majority of women, for reasons that I shall presently expose, were not eager for the extension, and regard it as of small value today. They know that they can get what they want without going to the actual polls for it; moreover, they are out of sympathy with most of the brummagem reforms advocated by the professional suffragists, male and female. The mere statement of the current suffragist platform, with its long list of quack sure-cures for all the sorrows of the world, is enough to make them smile sadly. In particular, they are

sceptical of all reforms that depend upon the mass
action of immense numbers of voters, large sections
of whom are wholly devoid of sense. A normal woman,
indeed, no more believes in democracy in the nation than she believes in democracy at her own
fireside; she knows that there must be a class to
order and a class to obey, and that the two can never
coalesce. Nor is she susceptible to the stock sentimentalities upon which the whole democratic process
is based. This was shown very dramatically in the
United States at the national election of 1920, in which
the late Woodrow Wilson was brought down to
colossal and ignominious defeat—the first general election in which all American women could vote. All
the sentimentality of the situation was on the side of
Wilson, and yet fully three-fourths of the newly-
enfranchised women voters voted against him. He is,
despite his talents for deception, a poor popular psychologist, and so he made an inept effort to fetch the
girls by tear-squeezing: every connoisseur will remember his bathos about breaking the heart of the world.
Well, very few women believe in broken hearts, and
the cause is not far to seek: practically every woman
above the age of twenty-five *has* a broken heart. That
is to say, she has been vastly disappointed, either by
failing to nab some pretty fellow that her heart was
set on, or, worse, by actually nabbing him, and then
discovering him to be a bounder or an imbecile, or
both. Thus walking the world with broken hearts,
women know that the injury is not serious. When he
pulled out the *Vox angelica* stop and began sobbing

and snuffling and blowing his nose tragically, the learned doctor simply drove all the women voters into the arms of the Hon. Warren Gamaliel Harding, who was too stupid to invent any issues at all, but simply took negative advantage of the distrust aroused by his opponent.

Once the women of Christendom become at ease in the use of the ballot, and get rid of the preposterous harridans who got it for them and who now seek to tell them what to do with it, they will proceed to a scotching of many of the sentimentalities which currently corrupt politics. For one thing, I believe that they will initiate measures against democracy—the worst evil of the present-day world. When they come to the matter, they will certainly not ordain the extension of the suffrage to children, criminals and the insane—in brief, to those even more inflammable and knavish than the male hinds who have enjoyed it for so long; they will try to bring about its restriction, bit by bit, to the small minority that is intelligent, agnostic and self-possessed—say six women to one man. Thus, out of their greater instinct for reality, they will make democracy safe for a democracy.

The curse of man, and the cause of nearly all his woes, is his stupendous capacity for believing the incredible. He is forever embracing delusions, and each new one is worse than all that have gone before. But where is the delusion that women cherish—I mean habitually, firmly, passionately? Who will draw up a list of propositions, held and maintained by them in sober earnest, that are obviously not true? (I allude here, of course, to genuine women, not to suffragettes and other such pseudo-males). As for me, I should not like to undertake such a list. I know of nothing, in fact, that properly belongs to it. Women, as a class, believe in none of the ludicrous rights, duties and pious obligations that men are forever gabbling about. Their superior intelligence is in no way more eloquently demonstrated than by their ironical view of all such phantasmagoria. Their habitual attitude toward men is one of aloof disdain, and their habitual attitude toward what men believe in, and get into sweats about, and bellow for, is substantially the same. It takes twice as long to convert a body of women to some new fallacy as it takes to convert a body of men, and even then they halt, hesitate and are full of mordant criticisms. The women of Colorado had been voting for 21 years before they succumbed to prohibition sufficiently to allow the man voters of the state to adopt it; their own majority voice was against it to the end. During the interval the men voters of a dozen non-suffrage American states had gone shrieking to the mourners' bench. In California, enfranchised in 1911, the women rejected the dry revelation in 1914. National prohibition was adopted during the war without their votes—they did not get the franchise throughout the country until it was in the Constitution—and it is without their support today. The American man, despite his reputation for lawlessness, is actually very much afraid of the police, and in all the regions where prohibition is now actually enforced he makes excuses for his poltroonish acceptance of it by arguing that it will do him good in the long run, or that he ought to sacrifice his private desires to the common weal. But it is almost impossible to find an American woman of any culture who is in favour of it. One and all, they are opposed to the turmoil and corruption that it involves, and resentful of the invasion of liberty underlying it. Being realists, they have no belief in any program which proposes to cure the natural swinishness of men by legislation. Every normal woman believes, and quite accurately, that the average man is very much like her husband, John, and she knows very well that John is a weak, silly and knavish fellow, and that any effort to convert him into an archangel overnight is bound to come to grief. As for her view of the average creature of her own sex, it is marked by a cynicism so penetrating and so destructive that a clear statement of it would shock beyond endurance.

32. *The Woman Voter*

THUS THERE is not the slightest chance that the enfranchised women of Protestantdom, once they become at ease in the use of the ballot, will give any heed to the ex-suffragettes who now presume to lead and instruct them in politics. Years ago I predicted that these suffragettes, tried out by victory, would turn out to be idiots. They are now hard at work proving it. Half of them devote themselves to advocating reforms, chiefly of a sexual character, so utterly preposterous that even male politicians and newspaper editors laugh at them; the other half succumb absurdly to the blandishments of the old-time male politicians, and so enroll themselves in the great political parties. A woman who joins one of these parties simply becomes an imitation man, which is to say, a donkey. Thereafter she is nothing but an obscure cog in an ancient and creaking machine, the sole intelligible purpose of which is to maintain a horde of scoundrels in public office. Her vote is instantly set off by the vote of some sister who joins the other camorra. Parenthetically, I may add that all of the ladies to take to this political immolation seem to me to be frightfully plain. I know those of England, Germany and Scandinavia only by their portraits in the illustrated papers, but those of the United States I have studied at close range at various large political gatherings, including the two national conventions first following the extension of the suffrage. I am surely no fastidious fellow—in fact, I prefer a certain melancholy decay in women to the loud, circus-wagon brilliance of youth—but I give you my word that there were not five women at either national convention who could have embraced me in camera without first giving me chloral. Some of the chief stateswomen on show, in fact, were so downright hideous that I felt faint every time I had to look at them.

The reform-monging suffragists seem to be equally devoid of the more caressing gifts. They may be filled with altruistic passion, but they certainly have bad complexions, and not many of them know how to dress their hair. Nine-tenths of them advocate reforms aimed at the alleged lubricity of the male—the single standard, medical certificates for bridegrooms, birth-control, and so on. The motive here, I believe, is mere rage and jealousy. The woman who is not pursued sets up the doctrine that pursuit is offensive to her sex, and wants to make it a felony. No genuinely attractive woman has any such desire. She likes masculine admiration, however violently expressed, and is quite able to take care of herself. More, she is well aware that very few men are bold enough to offer it without a plain invitation, and this awareness makes her extremely cynical of all women who complain of being harassed, beset, stormed, and seduced. All the more intelligent women that I know, indeed, are unanimously of the opinion that no girl in her right senses has ever been actually seduced since the world began; whenever they hear of a case, they sympathize with the man. Yet more, the normal woman of lively charms, roving about among men, always tries to draw the admiration of those who have previously admired elsewhere; she prefers the professional to the amateur, and estimates her skill by the attractiveness of the huntresses who have hitherto stalked the game. The iron-faced suffragist propagandist, if she gets a man at all, must get one wholly without sentimental experience. If he has any, her crude manœuvres make him laugh and he is repelled by her lack of pulchritude and amiability. All such suffragists (save a few miraculous beauties) marry ninth-rate men when they marry at all. They have to put up with the sort of cast-offs who are almost ready to fall in love with lady physicists, embryologists, and embalmers.

Fortunately for the human race, the campaigns of these indignant viragoes will come to naught. Men will keep on pursuing women until hell freezes over, and women will keep luring them on. If the latter enterprise were abandoned, in fact, the whole game of love would play out, for not many men take any notice of women spontaneously. Nine men out of ten would be quite happy, I believe, if there were no women in the world, once they had grown accustomed to the quiet. Practically all men *are* their happiest when they are engaged upon activities—for example, drinking, gambling, hunting, business, adventure—to which women are not ordinarily admitted. It is women who seduce them from such celibate doings. The hare postures and gyrates in front of the hound. The way to put an end to the gaudy crimes that the suffragist alarmists talk about is to shave the heads of all the pretty girls in the world, and pluck out their eyebrows, and pull their teeth, and put them in khaki, and forbid them to wriggle on dance-floors, or to wear scents, or to use lip-sticks, or to roll their eyes. Reform, as usual, mistakes the fish for the fly.

33. A Glance Into the Future

THE PRESENT public pros-
perity of the exsuffragettes is chiefly due to the fact
that the old-time male politicians, being naturally
very stupid, mistake them for spokesmen for the
whole body of women, and so show them politeness.
But soon or late—and probably disconcertingly soon
—the great mass of sensible and agnostic women will
turn upon them and depose them, and thereafter the
woman vote will be no longer at the disposal of bogus
Great Thinkers and messiahs. If the suffragettes continue to fill the newspapers with nonsense, once that
change has been effected, it will be only as a minority
sect of tolerated idiots, like the Swedenborgians,
Christian Scientists, Seventh Day Adventists and other
such fanatics of today. This was the history of the
extension of the suffrage in all of the American states
that made it before the national enfranchisement of
women and it will be repeated in the nation at large,
and in Great Britain and on the Continent. Women
are not taken in by quackery as readily as men are;
the hardness of their shell of logic makes it difficult
to penetrate to their emotions. For one woman who
testifies publicly that she has been cured of cancer by

some swindling patent medicine, there are at least twenty masculine witnesses. Even such frauds as the favourite American elixir, Lydia Pinkham's Vegetable Compound, which are ostensibly remedies for specifically feminine ills, anatomically impossible in the male, are chiefly swallowed, so an intelligent druggist tells me, by men.

My own belief, based on elaborate inquiries and long meditation, is that the grant of the ballot to women marks the concealed but none the less real beginning of an improvement in our politics, and, in the end, in our whole theory of government. As things stand, an intelligent grappling with some of the capital problems of the commonwealth is almost impossible. A politician normally prospers under democracy, not in proportion as his principles are sound and his honour incorruptible, but in proportion as he excels in the manufacture of sonorous phrases, and the invention of imaginary perils and imaginary defences against them. Our politics thus degenerates into a mere pursuit of hobgoblins; the male voter, a coward as well as an ass, is forever taking fright at a new one and electing some mountebank to lay it. For a hundred years past the people of the United States, the most terrible existing democratic state, have scarcely had a political campaign that was not based upon some preposterous fear—first of slavery and then of the manumitted slave, first of capitalism and then of communism, first of the old and then of the novel. It is a peculiarity of women that they are not easily set off by such alarms, that they do not fall readily into such facile

tumults and phobias. What starts a male meeting to
snuffling and trembling most violently is precisely the
thing that would cause a female meeting to sniff.
What we need, to ward off mobocracy and safeguard
a civilized form of government, is more of this sniffing.
What we need—and in the end it must come—is a
sniff so powerful that it will call a halt upon the navi-
gation of the ship from the forecastle, and put a competent staff on the bridge, and lay a course that is
describable in intelligible terms.

The officers nominated by the male electorate in
modern democracies before the extension of the suffrage
were usually chosen, not for their competence but for
their mere talent for idiocy; they reflected accurately
the male weakness for whatever is rhetorical and sentimental and feeble and untrue. Consider, for example,
what happened in a salient case. Every four years the
male voters of the United States chose from among
themselves one who was put forward as the man most
fit, of all resident men, to be the first citizen of the
commonwealth. He was chosen after interminable discussion; his qualifications were thoroughly can-
vassed; very large powers and dignities were put into
his hands. Well, what did we commonly find when we
examined this gentleman? We found, not a profound
thinker, not a leader of sound opinion, not a man of
notable sense, but merely a wholesaler of notions so infantile that they must needs disgust a sentient suckling
—in brief, a spouting geyser of fallacies and sentimentalities, a cataract of unsupported assumptions and
hollow moralizings, a tedious phrase-merchant and

platitudinarian, a fellow whose noblest flights of thought were flattered when they were called comprehensible—specifically, a Wilson, a Taft, a Roosevelt, or a Harding.

This was the male champion. I do not venture upon the cruelty of comparing his bombastic flummeries to the clear reasoning of a woman of like fame and position; all I ask of you is that you weigh them, for sense, for shrewdness, for intelligent grasp of obscure relations, for intellectual honesty and courage, with the ideas of the average midwife.

34. The Suffragette

I HAVE SPOKEN with some disdain of the suffragette. What is the matter with her, fundamentally, is simple: she is a woman who has stupidly carried her envy of certain of the superficial privileges of men to such a point that it takes on the character of an obsession, and makes her blind to their valueless and often chiefly imaginary character. In particular, she centres this frenzy of hers upon one definite privilege, to wit, the alleged privilege of promiscuity in amour, the modern *droit du seigneur*. Read the books of the chief lady Savonarolas, and you will find running through them an hysterical denunciation of what is called the double standard of morality; there is, indeed, a whole literature devoted exclusively to it. The existence of this double standard seems to drive the poor girls half frantic. They bellow raucously for its abrogation, and demand that the frivolous male be visited with even more idiotic penalties than those which now visit the aberrant female; some even advocate gravely his mutilation by surgery, that he may be forced into rectitude by a physical disability for sin.

All this, of course, is hocus-pocus, and the judicious are not deceived by it for an instant. What these virtuous beldames actually desire in their hearts is not that the male be reduced to chemical purity, but that the franchise of dalliance be extended to themselves. The most elementary acquaintance with Freudian psychology exposes their secret animus. Unable to ensnare males under the present system, or at all events, unable to ensnare males sufficiently appetizing to arouse the envy of other women, they leap to the theory that it would be easier if the rules were less exacting. This theory exposes their deficiency in the chief character of their sex: accurate observation. The fact is that, even if they possessed the freedom that men are supposed to possess, they would still find it difficult to achieve their ambition, for the average man, whatever his stupidity, is at least keen enough in judgment to prefer a single wink from a genuinely attractive woman to the last delirious favours of the typical suffragette. Thus the theory of the whoopers and snorters of the cause, in its esoteric as well as in its public aspect, is unsound. They are simply women who, in their tastes and processes of mind, are two-thirds men, and the fact explains their failure to achieve presentable husbands, or even con-solatory betrayal, quite as effectively as it explains the ready credence they give to political and philosophical absurdities.

35. A Mythical Dare-Devil

HE TRUTH is that the pic-ture of male carnality that such women conjure up belongs almost wholly to fable, as I have already ob-served in dealing with the sophistries of Dr. Eliza Burt Gamble, a paralogist on a somewhat higher plane. As they depict him in their fevered treatises on illegiti-macy, white-slave trading and *ophthalmia neona-torum* the average male adult of the Christian and cultured countries leads a life of gaudy lubricity, rolling magnificently from one liaison to another, and with an almost endless queue of ruined milliners, dancers, charwomen, parlour-maids and waitresses behind him, all dying of poison and despair. The life of man, as these furiously envious ones see it, is the life of a lead-ing actor in a boulevard *revue*. He is a polygamous, multigamous, myriadigamous; an insatiable and un-

conscionable débauché, a monster of promiscuity; pro-
digiously unfaithful to his wife, and even to his friends'
wives; fathomlessly libidinous and superbly happy.

Needless to say, this picture bears no more relation
to the facts than a dissertation on major strategy by
a military "expert" promoted from dramatic critic. If
the chief suffragette scare mongers (I speak without
any embarrassing naming of names) were attractive
enough to men to get near enough to enough men to
know enough about them for their purpose they would
paralyze the Dorcas societies with no such cajoling
libels. As a matter of sober fact, the average man of
our time and race is quite incapable of all these in-
candescent and intriguing divertisements. He is far
more virtuous than they make him out, far less schooled
in sin, far less enterprising and ruthless. I do not say,
of course, that he is pure in heart, for the chances are
that he isn't; what I do say is that, in the overwhelming majority of cases, he is pure in act, even in the face
of temptation. And why? For several main reasons,
not to go into minor ones. One is that he lacks the
courage. Another is that he lacks the money. Another
is that he is fundamentally moral, and has a conscience.
It takes more sinful initiative than he has in him to
plunge into any affair save the most casual and sordid;
it takes more ingenuity and intrepidity than he has in
him to carry it off; it takes more money than he can
conceal from his consort to finance it. A man may force
his actual wife to share the direst poverty, but even the
least vampirish woman of the third part demands to
be courted in what, considering his station in life, is

the grand manner, and the expenses of that grand manner scare off all save a small minority of specialists in deception. So long, indeed, as a wife knows her husband's income accurately, she has a sure means of holding him to his oaths.

Even more effective than the fiscal barrier is the barrier of poltroonery. The one character that distinguishes man from the other higher vertebrata, indeed, is his excessive timorousness, his easy yielding to alarms, his incapacity for adventure without a crowd behind him. In his normal incarnation he is no more capable of initiating an extra-legal affair—at all events, above the mawkish harmlessness of a flirting match with a cigar girl in a café—than he is of scaling the battlements of hell. He likes to think of himself doing it, just as he likes to think of himself leading a cavalry charge or climbing the Matterhorn. Often, indeed, his vanity leads him to imagine the thing done, and he admits by winks and blushes that he is a bad one. But at the bottom of all that tawdry pretence there is usually nothing more material than an oafish smirk at some disgusted shop-girl, or a scraping of shins under the table. Let any woman who is disquieted by reports of her husband's derelictions figure to herself how long it would have taken him to propose to her if left to his own enterprise, and then let her ask herself if so pusillanimous a creature could be imagined in the rôle of Don Giovanni.

Finally, there is his conscience—the accumulated sediment of ancestral faint-heartedness in countless generations, with vague religious fears and superstitions

to leaven and mellow it. What! a conscience? Yes, dear
friends, a conscience. That conscience may be imperfect, inept, unintelligent, brummagem. It may be indistinguishable, at times, from the mere fear that some
one may be looking. It may be shot through with
hypocrisy, stupidity, play-acting. But nevertheless, as
consciences go in Christendom, it is genuinely entitled
to the name—and it is always in action. A man, remember, is not a being *in vacuo;* he is the fruit and
slave of the environment that bathes him. One cannot
enter the House of Commons, the United States Sen-
ate, or a prison for felons without becoming, in some
measure, a rascal. One cannot fall overboard without
shipping water. One cannot pass through a modern
university without carrying away scars. And by the
same token one cannot live and have one's being in a
modern democratic state, year in and year out, without
falling, to some extent at least, under that moral obsession which is the hall-mark of the mob-man set free.
A citizen of such a state, his nose buried in Nietzsche,
"Man and Superman," and other such advanced literature, may caress himself with the notion that he is an
immoralist, that his soul is full of soothing sin, that he
has cut himself loose from the revelation of God. But
all the while there is a part of him that remains a sound
Christian, a moralist, a right-thinking and forward-
looking man. And that part, in times of stress, asserts
itself. It may not worry him on ordinary occasions. It
may not stop him when he swears, or takes a nip of
whiskey behind the door, or goes motoring on Sunday;
it may even let him alone when he goes to a leg-show.
But the moment a concrete Temptress rises before him,

her nose snow-white, her lips rouged, her eyelashes drooping provokingly—the moment such an abandoned wench has at him, and his lack of ready funds begins to conspire with his lack of courage to assault and wobble him—at that precise moment his conscience flares into function, and so finishes his business. First he sees difficulty, then he sees danger, then he sees wrong. The result? The result is that he slinks off in trepidation, and another vampire is baffled of her prey.

It is, indeed, the secret scandal of Christendom, at least in the Protestant regions, that most men are faithful to their wives. You will travel a long way before you find a married man who will admit that *he* is, but the facts are the facts, and I am surely not one to flout them.

36. *The Origin of a Delusion*

THE ORIGIN of the delusion that the average man is a Leopold II or Augustus the Strong, with the amorous experience of a guinea pig, is not far to seek. It lies in three factors, the which I rehearse briefly:

1. The idiotic vanity of men, leading to their eternal boasting, either by open lying or sinister hints.
2. The notions of vice crusaders, nonconformist divines,

Y.M.C.A. secretaries, and other such libidinous poltroons as to what they would do themselves if they had the courage.

3. The ditto of certain suffragettes as to ditto ditto.

Here you have the genesis of a generalization that gives the less critical sort of women a great deal of needless uneasiness and vastly augments the natural conceit of men. Some pornographic old fellow, in the discharge of his duties as director of an anti-vice society, puts in an evening ploughing through such books as "The Memoirs of Fanny Hill," Casanova's Confessions, the Cena Trimalchionis of Gaius Petronius, and II Samuel. From this perusal he arises with the conviction that life amid the red lights must be one stupendous whirl of deviltry, that the clerks he sees in Broadway or Piccadilly at night are out for revels that would have caused protests in Sodom and Nineveh, that the average man who chooses hell leads an existence comparable to that of a Mormon bishop, that the world outside the Bible class is packed like a sardine-can with betrayed salesgirls, that every man who doesn't believe that Jonah swallowed the whale spends his whole leisure leaping through the seventh hoop of the Decalogue. "If I were not saved and anointed of God," whispers the vice director into his own ear, "that is what I, the Rev. Dr. Jasper Barebones, would be doing. The late King David did it; he was human, and hence immoral. The late King Edward VII was not beyond suspicion: the very numeral in his name has its suggestions. Millions of others go the same route. . . . *Ergo,* Up, guards, and at em! Bring me the pad of blank warrants! Order out the searchlights and scaling-ladders! Swear in four hundred more policemen! Let us chase these hell-hounds out of Christendom, and make the world safe for monogamy, poor working girls, and infant damnation!"

Thus the hound of heaven, arguing fallaciously from his own secret aspirations. Where he makes his mistake is in assuming that the unconsecrated, while sharing his longing to debauch and betray, are free from his other weaknesses, *e. g.,* his timidity, his lack of resourcefulness, his conscience. As I have said, they are not. The vast majority of those who appear in the public haunts of sin are there, not to engage in overt acts of ribaldry, but merely to tremble agreeably upon the edge of the abyss. They are the same skittish experimentalists, precisely, who throng the midway at a world's fair, and go to smutty shows, and take in sex magazines, and read the sort of books that our vice-crusading friend reads. They like to conjure up the charms of carnality, and to help out their somewhat sluggish imaginations by actual peeps at it, but when it comes to taking a forthright header into the sulphur they usually fail to muster up the courage. For one clerk who succumbs to the houris of the pave, there are five hundred who succumb to lack of means, the warnings of the sex hygienists, and their own depressing consciences. For one "clubman"—*i. e.,* bagman or suburban vestryman—who invades the women's shops, engages the affection of some innocent miss, lures her

into infamy and then sells her to the Italians, there are
one thousand who never get any further than asking
the price of cologne water and discharging a few fur-
tive winks. And for one husband of the Nordic race
who maintains a blonde chorus girl in oriental luxury
around the corner, there are ten thousand who are as
true to their wives, year in and year out, as so many
convicts in the death-house, and would be no more
capable of any such loathsome malpractice, even in the
face of free opportunity, than they would be of cutting
off the ears of their young.

I am sorry to blow up so much romance. In particular, I am sorry for the suffragettes who specialize in
the double standard, for when they get into pantaloons
at last, and have the new freedom, they will discover
to their sorrow that they have been pursuing a chimera
—that there is really no such animal as the male
anarchist they have been denouncing and envying—
that the wholesale fornication of man, at least under
Christian democracy, has little more actual existence
than honest advertising or sound cooking. They have
followed the pornomaniacs in embracing a piece of
buncombe, and when the day of deliverance comes it
will turn to ashes in their arms.

Their error, as I say, lies in overestimating the
courage and enterprise of man. They themselves, bar-
ring mere physical valour, a quality in which the average man is far exceeded by the average jackal or wolf,
have more of both. If the consequences, to a man, of the
slightest descent from virginity were one-tenth as
swift and barbarous as the consequences to a young
girl in like case, it would take a division of infantry

to dredge up a single male flouter of that *lex talionis* in the whole western world. As things stand today, even with the odds so greatly in his favour, the average male hesitates and is thus not lost. Turn to the statistics of the vice crusaders if you doubt it. They show that the weekly receipts of female recruits upon the wharves of sin are always more than the demand; that more young women enter upon the vermilion career than can make respectable livings at it; that the pressure of the temptation they hold out is the chief factor in corrupting our undergraduates. What was the first act of the American Army when it began summoning its young clerks and college boys and plough hands to conscription camps? Its first act was to mark off a so-called moral zone around each camp, and to secure it with trenches and machine guns, and to put a lot of volunteer termagants to patrolling it, that the assembled *jeunesse* might be protected in their rectitude from the immoral advances of the adjacent milkmaids and poor working girls.

37. *Women as Martyrs*

I HAVE GIVEN three reasons for the prosperity of the notion that man is a natural polygamist, bent eternally upon fresh dives into Lake of Brimstone No. 7. To these another should be added:

the thirst for martyrdom which shows itself in so many women, particularly under the higher forms of civilization. This unhealthy appetite, in fact, may be described as one of civilization's diseases; it is almost unheard of in more primitive societies. The savage woman, unprotected by her rude culture and forced to heavy and incessant labour, has retained her physical strength and with it her honesty and self-respect. The civilized woman, gradually degenerated by a greater ease, and helped down that hill by the pretensions of civilized man, has turned her infirmity into a virtue, and so affects a feebleness that is actually far beyond the reality. It is by this route that she can most effectively disarm masculine distrust, and get what she wants. Man is flattered by any acknowledgement, however insincere, of his superior strength and capacity. He likes to be leaned upon, appealed to, followed docilely. And this tribute to his might caresses him on the psychic plane as well as on the plane of the obviously physical. He not only enjoys helping a woman over a gutter; he also enjoys helping her dry her tears. The result is the vast pretence that characterizes the relations of the sexes under civilization—the double pretence of man's cunning and autonomy and of woman's dependence and deference. Man is always looking for some one to boast to; woman is always looking for a shoulder to put her head on.

This feminine affectation, of course, has gradually taken on the force of a fixed habit, and so it has got a certain support, by a familiar process of self-delusion, in reality. The civilized woman inherits that habit as she inherits her cunning. She is born half convinced that she is really as weak and helpless as she later pretends to be, and the prevailing folklore offers her endless corroboration. One of the resultant phenomena is the delight in martyrdom that one so often finds in women, and particularly in the least alert and introspective of them. They take a heavy, unhealthy pleasure in suffering; it subtly pleases them to be hard put upon; they like to picture themselves as slaughtered saints. Thus they always find something to complain of; the very conditions of domestic life give them a superabundance of clinical material. And if, by any chance, such material shows a falling off, they are uneasy and unhappy. Let a woman have a husband whose conduct is not reasonably open to question, and she will invent mythical offences to make him bearable. And if her invention fails she will be plunged into the utmost misery and humiliation. This fact probably explains many mysterious divorces: the husband was not too bad, but too good. For public opinion among women, remember, does not favour the woman who is full of a placid contentment and has no masculine torts to report; if she says that her husband is wholly satisfactory she is looked upon as a numskull even more dense than he is himself. A man, speaking of his wife to other men, always praises her extravagantly. Boasting about her soothes his vanity; he likes to stir up the envy of his fellows. But when two women talk of their husbands it is mainly atrocities that they describe. The most esteemed woman gossip is the one with the longest and most various repertoire of complaints.

This yearning for martyrdom explains one of the commonly noted characters of women: their eager flair for bearing physical pain. As we have seen, they have actually a good deal less endurance than men; massive injuries shock them more severely and kill them more quickly. But when acute algesia is unaccompanied by any profounder phenomena they are undoubtedly able to bear it with a far greater show of resignation. The reason is not far to seek. In pain a man sees only an invasion of his liberty, strength and self-esteem. It floors him, masters him, and makes him ridiculous. But a woman, more subtle and devious in her processes of mind, senses the dramatic effect that the spectacle of her suffering makes upon the spectators, already filled with compassion for her feebleness. She would thus much rather be praised for facing pain with a martyr's fortitude than for devising some means of getting rid of it—the first thought of a man. No woman could have invented chloroform, nor, for that matter, alcohol. Both drugs offer an escape from situations and experiences that, even in aggravated forms, women relish. The woman who drinks as men drink —that is, to raise her threshold of sensation and ease the agony of living—nearly always shows a deficiency in feminine characters and an undue preponderance of masculine characters. Almost invariably you will find her vain and boastful, and full of other marks of that bombastic exhibitionism which is so sterlingly male.

38. Pathological Effects

THIS FEMININE craving for martyrdom, of course, often takes on a downright pathological character, and so engages the psychiatrist. Women show many other traits of the same sort. To be a woman under our Christian civilization, indeed, means to live a life that is heavy with repression and dissimulation, and this repression and dissimulation, in the long run, cannot fail to produce effects that are indistinguishable from disease. You will find some of them described at length in any handbook on psychoanalysis. The Viennese, Adler, and the Dane, Poul Bjerre, argue, indeed, that womanliness itself, as it is encountered under Christianity, is a disease. All women suffer from a suppressed revolt against the inhibitions forced upon them by our artificial culture, and this suppressed revolt, by well known Freudian means, produces a complex of mental symptoms that is familiar to all of us. At one end of the scale we observe the suffragette, with her grotesque adoption of the male belief in laws, phrases and talismans, and her hysterical demand for a sexual libertarianism that she could not put to use if she had it. And at the other end we find the snuffling and neurotic woman, with her bogus

martyrdom, her extravagant pruderies and her pathological delusions. As Ibsen observed long ago, this is a
man's world. Women have broken many of their old
chains, but they are still enmeshed in a formidable
network of man-made taboos and sentimentalities, and
it will take them another generation, at least, to get
genuine freedom. That this is true is shown by the
deep unrest that yet marks the sex, despite its recent
progress toward social, political and economic equality.
It is almost impossible to find a man who honestly
wishes that he were a woman, but almost every woman,
at some time or other in her life, is gnawed by a regret
that she is not a man.

Two of the hardest things that women have to bear
are (a) the stupid masculine disinclination to admit
their intellectual superiority, or even their equality, or
even their possession of a normal human equipment
for thought, and (b) the equally stupid masculine doctrine that they constitute a special and ineffable species
of vertebrata, without the natural instincts and appetites of the order—to adapt a phrase from Haeckel,
that they are transcendental and almost gaseous mammals, and marked by a complete lack of certain salient
mammalian characters. The first imbecility has already
concerned us at length. One finds traces of it even in
works professedly devoted to disposing of it. In one
such book, for example, I come upon this: "What all
the skill and constructive capacity of the physicians in
the Crimean War failed to accomplish Florence
Nightingale accomplished by her beautiful femininity
and nobility of soul." In other words, by her possession

of some recondite and indescribable magic, sharply separated from the ordinary mental processes of man. The theory is unsound and preposterous. Miss Nightingale accomplished her useful work, not by magic, but by hard common sense. The problem before her was simply one of organization. Many men had tackled it, and all of them had failed stupendously. What she did was to bring her feminine sharpness of wit, her feminine clear-thinking, to bear upon it. Thus attacked, it yielded quickly, and once it had been brought to order it was easy for other persons to carry on what she had begun. But the opinion of a man's world still prefers to credit her success to some mysterious angelical quality, unstatable in lucid terms and having no more reality than the divine inspiration of an archbishop. Her extraordinarily acute and accurate intelligence is thus conveniently put upon the table, and the *amour propre* of man is kept inviolate. To confess frankly that she had more sense than any male Englishman of her generation would be to utter a truth too harsh to be bearable.

The second delusion commonly shows itself in the theory, already discussed, that women are devoid of any sex instinct—that they submit to the odious caresses of the lubricious male only by a powerful effort of the will, and with the sole object of discharging their duty to posterity. It would be impossible to go into this delusion with proper candour and at due length in a work designed for reading aloud in the domestic circle; all I can do is to refer the student to the books of any competent authority on the psychology of sex, say Ellis, or to the confidences (if they are obtainable) of any complaisant bachelor of his acquaintance.

39. Women as Christians

THE GLAD TIDINGS preached by Christ were obviously highly favourable to women. He lifted them to equality before the Lord when their very possession of souls was still doubted by the majority of rival theologians. Moreover, He esteemed them socially and set value upon their sagacity, and one of the most disdained of their sex, a lady formerly in public life, was among His regular advisers. Mariolatry is thus by no means the invention of the mediaeval popes, as Protestant theologians would have us believe. On the contrary, it is plainly discernible in the Four Gospels. What the mediaeval popes actually invented (or, to be precise, reinvented, for they simply borrowed the elements of it from St. Paul) was the doctrine of women's inferiority, the precise opposite of the thing credited to them. Committed, for sound reasons of discipline, to the celibacy of the clergy, they had to support it by depicting all traffic with women in the light of a hazardous and ignominious business. The result was the deliberate organization and development of the theory of female triviality, lack of responsibility and

general looseness of mind. Woman became a sort of
devil, but without the admired intelligence of the regular demons. The appearance of women saints, however,
offered a constant and embarrassing criticism of this
idiotic doctrine. If occasional women were fit to sit
upon the right hand of God—and they were often
proving it, and forcing the church to acknowledge it—
then surely *all* women could not be as bad as the books
made them out. There thus arose the concept of the
angelic woman, the natural vestal; we see her at full
length in the romances of mediaeval chivalry. What
emerged in the end was a sort of double doctrine, first
that women were devils and secondly that they were
angels. This preposterous dualism has merged, as we
have seen, into a compromise dogma in modern times.
By that dogma it is held, on the one hand, that women
are unintelligent and immoral, and on the other hand,
that they are free from all those weaknesses of the
flesh which distinguish men. This, roughly speaking,
is the notion of the average male numskull today.

Christianity has thus both libelled women and
flattered them, but with the weight always on the side
of the libel. It is therefore, at bottom, their enemy, as
the religion of Christ, now wholly extinct, was their
friend. And as they gradually throw off the shackles
that have bound them for a thousand years they show
appreciation of the fact. Women, indeed, are not naturally religious, and they are growing less and less religious as year chases year. Their ordinary devotion has
little if any pious exaltation in it; it is a routine practice, forced on them by the masculine notion that an

appearance of holiness is proper to their lowly station, and a masculine feeling that church-going somehow keeps them in order, and out of doings that would be less reassuring. When they exhibit any genuine religious fervour, its sexual character is usually so obvious that even the majority of men are cognizant of it. Women never go flocking ecstatically to a church in which the agent of God in the pulpit is an elderly asthmatic with a watchful wife. When one finds them driven to frenzies by the merits of the saints, and weeping over the sorrows of the heathen, and rushing out to haul the whole vicinage up to grace, and spending hours on their knees in hysterical abasement before the heavenly throne, it is quite safe to assume, even without an actual visit, that the ecclesiastic who has worked the miracle is a fair and toothsome fellow, and a good deal more aphrodisiacal than learned. All the great preachers to women in modern times have been men of suave and ingratiating habit, and the great majority of them, from Henry Ward Beecher up and down, have been taken, soon or late, in transactions far more suitable to the boudoir than to the footstool of the Almighty. Their famous killings have always been made among the silliest sort of women—the sort, in brief, who fall so short of the normal acumen of their sex that they are bemused by mere beauty in men.

Such women are in a minority, and so the sex shows a good deal fewer religious enthusiasts *per mille* than the sex of sentiment and belief. Attending, several years ago, the gladiatorial shows of the Rev. Dr. Billy Sunday, the celebrated American pulpit-clown, I was constantly struck by the great preponderance of males in the pen devoted to the saved. Men of all ages and in enormous numbers came swarming to the altar, loudly bawling for help against their sins, but the women were anything but numerous, and the few who appeared were chiefly either chlorotic adolescents or pathetic old *Saufschwestern*. For six nights running I sat directly beneath the gifted exhorter without seeing a single female convert of what statisticians call the child-bearing age—that is, the age of maximum intelligence and charm. Among the male simpletons bagged by his yells during this time were the president of a railroad, half a dozen rich bankers and merchants, and the former governor of an American state. But not a woman of comparable position or dignity. Not a woman that any self-respecting bachelor would care to chuck under the chin.

This cynical view of religious emotionalism, and with it of the whole stock of ecclesiastical balderdash, is probably responsible, at least in part, for the reluctance of women to enter upon the sacerdotal career. In those Christian sects which still bar them from the pulpit—usually on the imperfectly concealed ground that they are not equal to its alleged demands upon the morals and the intellect—one never hears of them protesting against the prohibition; they are quite content to leave the degrading imposture to men, who are better fitted for it by talent and conscience. And in those baroque sects, chiefly American, which admit them they show no eagerness to put on the stole and chasuble. When the first clergywoman appeared in the

United States, it was predicted by alarmists that men would be driven out of the pulpit by the new competition. Nothing of the sort has occurred, nor is it in prospect. The whole corps of female divines in the country might be herded into one small room. Women, when literate at all, are far too intelligent to make effective ecclesiastics. Their sharp sense of reality is in endless opposition to the whole sacerdotal masquerade, and their cynical humour stands against the snorting that is inseparable from pulpit oratory.

Those women who enter upon the religious life are almost invariably moved by some motive distinct from mere pious inflammation. It is a commonplace, indeed, that, in Catholic countries, girls are driven into convents by economic considerations or by disasters of amour far oftener than they are drawn there by the hope of heaven. Read the lives of the female saints, and you will see how many of them tried marriage and failed at it before ever they turned to religion. In Protestant lands very few women adopt it as a profession at all, and among the few a secular impulse is almost always visible. The girl who is suddenly overcome by a desire to minister to the heathen in foreign lands is nearly invariably found, on inspection, to be a girl harbouring a theory that it would be agreeable to marry some heroic missionary. In point of fact, she duly marries him. At home, perhaps, she has found it impossible to get a husband, but in the remoter marches of China, Senegal and Somaliland, with no white competition present, it is equally impossible to fail.

HAT REMAINS of the alleged piety of women is little more than a social habit, reinforced in most communities by a paucity of other and more inviting divertissements. If you have ever observed the women of Spain and Italy at their devotions you need not be told how much the worship of God may be a mere excuse for relaxation and gossip. These women, in their daily lives, are surrounded by a formidable network of mediaeval taboos; their normal human desire for ease and freedom in intercourse is opposed by masculine distrust and superstition; they meet no strangers; they see and hear nothing new. In the house of the Most High they escape from that vexing routine. Here they may brush shoulders with a crowd. Here, so to speak, they may crane their mental necks and stretch their spiritual legs. Here, above all, they may come into some sort of contact with men relatively more affable, cultured and charming than their husbands and fathers—to wit, with the rev. clergy.

Elsewhere in Christendom, though women are not quite so relentlessly watched and penned up, they feel much the same need of variety and excitement, and both are likewise on tap in the temples of the Lord. No one, I am sure, need be told that the average missionary society or church sewing circle is not primarily a religious organization. Its actual purpose is precisely that of the absurd clubs and secret orders to which the lower and least resourceful classes of men belong: it offers a means of refreshment, of self-expression, of personal display, of political manipulation and boasting, and, if the pastor happens to be interesting, of discreet and almost lawful intrigue. In the course of a life largely devoted to the study of pietistic phenomena, I have never met a single woman who cared an authentic damn for the actual heathen. The attraction in their salvation is always almost purely social. Women go to church for the same reason that farmers and convicts go to church.

Finally, there is the aesthetic lure. Religion, in most parts of Christendom, holds out the only bait of beauty that the inhabitants are ever cognizant of. It offers music, dim lights, relatively ambitious architecture, eloquence, formality and mystery, the caressing meaninglessness that is at the heart of poetry. Women are far more responsive to such things than men, who are ordinarily quite as devoid of aesthetic sensitiveness as so many oxen. The attitude of the typical man toward beauty in its various forms is, in fact, an attitude of suspicion and hostility. He does not regard a work of art as merely inert and stupid; he regards it as, in some indefinable way, positively offensive. He sees the artist as a professional voluptuary and scoundrel, and would no more trust him in his household than he would trust a coloured clergy-man in his hen-yard. It was men, and not women, who invented such sordid and literal faiths as those of the Mennonites, Dunkards, Wesleyans and Scotch Presbyterians, with their antipathy to beautiful ritual, their obscene buttonholing of God, their great talent for reducing the ineffable mystery of religion to a mere bawling of idiots. The normal woman, in so far as she has any religion at all, moves irresistibly toward Catholicism, with its poetical obscurantism. The evangelical Protestant sects have a hard time holding her. She can no more be an actual Methodist than a gentleman can be a Methodist.

This inclination toward beauty, of course, is dismissed by the average male blockhead as no more than a feeble sentimentality. The truth is that it is precisely the opposite. It is surely not sentimentality to be moved by the stately and mysterious ceremony of the mass, or even, say, by those timid imitations of it which one observes in certain Protestant churches. Such proceedings, whatever their defects from the standpoint of a pure aesthetic, are at all events vastly more beautiful than any of the private acts of the folk who take part in them. They lift themselves above the barren utilitarianism of everyday life, and no less above the maudlin sentimentalities that men seek pleasure in. They offer a means of escape, convenient and inviting, from that sordid routine of thought and occupation which women revolt against so pertinaciously.

HAVE SAID that the reli-
gion preached by Jesus (now wholly extinct in the
world) was highly favourable to women. This was not
saying, of course, that women have repaid the compliment by adopting it. They are, in fact, indifferent
Christians in the primitive sense, just as they are bad
Christians in the antagonistic modern sense, and particularly on the side of ethics. If they actually accept the
renunciations commanded by the Sermon on the Mount,
it is only in an effort to flout their substance under cover
of their appearance. No woman is really humble; she is
merely politic. No woman, with a free choice before
her, chooses self-immolation; the most she genuinely
desires in that direction is a spectacular martyrdom. No
woman delights in poverty. No woman yields when
she can prevail. No woman is honestly meek.

In their practical ethics, indeed, women pay little
heed to the precepts of the Founder of Christianity,
and the fact has passed into proverb. Their gentleness,
like the so-called honour of men, is visible only in
situations which offer them no menace. The moment a
woman finds herself confronted by an antagonist genuinely dangerous, either to her own security or to the

well-being of those under her protection—say a child
or a husband—she displays a bellicosity which stops at
nothing, however outrageous. In the courts of law one
occasionally encounters a male extremist who tells the
truth, the whole truth and nothing but the truth, even
when it is against his cause, but no such woman has
ever been on view since the days of Justinian. It is,
indeed, an axiom of the bar that women invariably
lie upon the stand, and the whole effort of a barrister
who has one for a client is devoted to keeping her within bounds, that the obtuse supsicions of the male jury
may not be unduly aroused. Women litigants almost
always win their cases, not, as is commonly assumed,
because the jurymen fall in love with them, but simply
and solely because they are clear-headed, resourceful,
implacable and without qualms.

What is here visible in the halls of justice, in the face
of a vast technical equipment for combating mendacity,
is ten times more obvious in freer fields. Any man who
is so unfortunate as to have a serious controversy
with a woman, say in the departments of finance,
theology or amour, must inevitably carry away from it
a sense of having passed through a dangerous and
almost gruesome experience. Women not only bite in
the clinches; they bite even in open fighting; they have
a dental reach, so to speak, of amazing length. No
attack is so desperate that they will not undertake it,
once they are aroused; no device is so unfair and
horrifying that it stays them. In my early days, desiring
to improve my prose, I served for a year or so as re-
porter for a newspaper in a police court, and during

that time I heard perhaps four hundred cases of so-
called wife-beating. The husbands, in their defence,
almost invariably pleaded justification, and some of
them told such tales of studied atrocity at the domestic hearth, both psychic and physical, that the learned
magistrate discharged them with tears in his eyes and
the very catchpolls in the courtroom had to blow their
noses. Many more men than women go insane, and
many more married men than single men. The fact
puzzles no one who has had the same opportunity
that I had to find out what goes on, year in and year
out, behind the doors of apparently happy homes. A
woman, if she hates her husband (and many of them
do), can make life so sour and obnoxious to him that
even death upon the gallows seems sweet by comparison. This hatred, of course, is often, and perhaps almost
invariably, quite justified. To be the wife of an ordinary
man, indeed, is an experience that must be very hard
to bear. The hollowness and vanity of the fellow, his
petty meanness and stupidity, his puling sentimentality
and credulity, his bombastic air of a cock on a dung-
hill, his anaesthesia to all whispers and summonings
of the spirit, above all, his loathsome clumsiness in
amour—all these things must revolt any woman above
the lowest. To be the object of the oafish affections of
such a creature, even when they are honest and profound, cannot be expected to give any genuine joy to a
woman of sense and refinement. His performance as a
gallant, as Honoré de Balzac long ago observed, unescapably suggests a gorilla's efforts to play the violin.
Women survive the tragi-comedy only by dint of

their great capacity for play-acting. They are able to act so realistically that often they deceive even themselves; the average woman's contentment, indeed, is no more than a tribute to her histrionism. But there must be innumerable revolts in secret, even so, and one sometimes wonders that so few women, with the thing so facile and so safe, poison their husbands. Perhaps it is not quite as rare as vital statistics make it out; the death rate among husbands is very much higher than among wives. More than once, indeed, I have gone to the funeral of an acquaintance who died suddenly, and observed a curious glitter in the eyes of the inconsolable widow.

Even in this age of emancipation, normal women have few serious transactions in life save with their husbands and potential husbands; the business of marriage is their dominant concern from adolescence to senility. When they step outside their habitual circle they show the same alert and eager wariness that they exhibit within it. A man who has dealings with them must keep his wits about him, and even when he is most cautious he is often flabbergasted by their sudden and unconscionable forays. Whenever a woman goes into trade she quickly gets a reputation as a sharp trader. Every little town in America has its Hetty Green, each sweating blood from turnips, each the terror of all the male usurers of the neighbourhood. The man who tackles such an amazon of barter takes his fortune into his hands; he has little more chance of success against the feminine technique in business than he has against the feminine technique in marriage. In both arenas the advantage of women lies in their freedom from sentimentality. In business they address themselves wholly to their own profit, and give no thought whatever to the hopes, aspirations and *amour propre* of their antagonists. And in the duel of sex they fence, not to make points, but to disable and disarm. A man, when he succeeds in throwing off a woman who has attempted to marry him, always carries away a maudlin sympathy for her in her defeat and dismay. But no one ever heard of a woman who pitied the poor fellow whose honest passion she had found it expedient to spurn. On the contrary, women take delight in such clownish agonies, and exhibit them proudly, and boast about them to other women.

V
THE
NEW
AGE

42. *The Transvaluation of Values*

HE GRADUAL emancipation of women that has been going on for the last century has still a long way to proceed before they are wholly delivered from their traditional burdens and so stand clear of the oppressions of men. But already, it must be plain, they have made enormous progress—perhaps more than they made in the ten thousand years preceding. The rise of the industrial system, which has borne so harshly upon the race in general, has brought them certain unmistakable benefits. Their economic dependence, though still sufficient to make marriage highly attractive to them, is nevertheless so far broken down that large classes of women are now almost free agents, and quite independent of the favour of men. Most of these women, responding to ideas that are still powerful, are yet intrigued, of course, by marriage, and prefer it to the autonomy that is coming in, but the fact remains that they now have a free choice in the matter, and that dire necessity no longer controls them. After all, they needn't marry if they don't want to; it is possible to get their bread by their own labour in the workshops of the world. Their grandmothers were in a far more difficult position. Failing marriage, they not only suffered a cruel ignominy, but in many cases faced the menace of actual starvation. There was simply no respectable place in the economy of those times for the free woman. She either had to enter a nunnery or accept a disdainful patronage that was as galling as charity.

Nothing could be plainer than the effect that the increasing economic security of women is having upon their whole habit of life and mind. The diminishing marriage rate and the even more rapidly diminishing birth rate show which way the wind is blowing. It is common for male statisticians, with characteristic imbecility, to ascribe the fall in the marriage rate to a growing disinclination on the male side. This growing disinclination is actually on the female side. Even though no considerable body of women has yet reached the definite doctrine that marriage is less desirable than freedom, it must be plain that large numbers of them now approach the business with far greater fastidiousness than their grandmothers or even their mothers exhibited. They are harder to please, and hence pleased less often. The woman of a century ago could imagine nothing more favourable to her than marriage; even marriage with a fifth-rate man was better than no marriage at all. This notion is gradually feeling the opposition of a contrary notion. Women in general may still prefer marriage to work, but there is an increasing minority which begins to realize that work may offer the greater contentment, particularly if it be mellowed by a certain amount of philandering.

There already appears in the world, indeed, a class of women, who, while still not genuinely averse to marriage, are yet free from any theory that it is necessary, or even invariably desirable. Among these women are a good many somewhat vociferous propagandists, almost male in their violent earnestness; they range from the man-eating suffragettes to such preachers of free motherhood as Ellen Key and such professional shockers of the bourgeoisie as the American prophetess of birth-control, Margaret Sanger. But among them are many more who wake the world with no such noisy eloquence, but content themselves with carrying out their ideas in a quiet and respectable manner. The number of such women is much larger than is generally imagined, and that number tends to increase steadily. They are women who, with their economic independence assured, either by inheritance or by their own efforts, chiefly in the arts and professions, do exactly as they please, and make no pother about it. Naturally enough, their superiority to convention and the common frenzy makes them extremely attractive to the better sort of men, and so it is not uncommon for one of them to find herself voluntarily sought in marriage, without any preliminary scheming by herself —surely an experience that very few ordinary women ever enjoy, save perhaps in dreams or delirium.

The old order changeth and giveth place to the new. Among the women's clubs and in the women's colleges, I have no doubt, there is still much debate of the old and silly question: Are platonic relations possible between the sexes? In other words, is friendship possible without sex? Many a woman of the new order dismisses the problem with another question: Why without sex? With the decay of the ancient concept of women as property there must come inevitably a reconsideration of the whole sex question, and out of that reconsideration there must come a revision of the mediaeval penalties which now punish the slightest frivolity in the female. The notion that honour in women is exclusively a physical matter, that a single aberrance may convert a woman of the highest merits into a woman of none at all, that the sole valuable thing a woman can bring to marriage is virginity—this notion is so preposterous that no intelligent person, male or female, actually cherishes it. It survives as one of the hollow conventions of Christianity; nay, of the levantine barbarism that preceded Christianity. As women throw off the other conventions which now bind them they will throw off this one, too, and so their virtue, grounded upon fastidiousness and self-respect instead of upon mere fear and conformity, will become a far more laudable thing than it ever can be under the present system. And for

its absence, if they see fit to dispose of it, they will no
more apologize than a man apologizes today.

43. *The Lady of Joy*

EVEN PROSTITUTION, in
the long run, may become a more or less respectable profession, as it was in the great days of the Greeks.
That quality will surely attach to it if ever it grows
quite unnecessary; whatever is unnecessary is always
respectable, for example, religion, fashionable clothing, and a knowledge of Latin grammar. The prostitute is disesteemed today, not because her trade
involves anything intrinsically degrading or even disagreeable, but because she is currently assumed to have
been driven into it by dire necessity, against her dignity
and inclination. That this assumption is usually unsound is no objection to it; nearly all the thinking of
the world, particularly in the field of morals, is based
upon unsound assumption, *e. g.,* that God observes
the fall of a sparrow and is shocked by the fall of a
Sunday-school superintendent. The truth is that
prostitution is one of the most attractive of the occupations practically open to the sort of women who

engage in it, and that the prostitute commonly likes her work, and would not exchange places with a shop-girl or a waitress for anything in the world. The notion to the contrary is propagated by unsuccessful prostitutes who fall into the hands of professional reformers, and who assent to the imbecile theories of the latter in order to cultivate their good will, just as convicts in prison, questioned by teetotalers, always ascribe their rascality to alcohol. No prostitute of anything resembling normal intelligence is under the slightest duress; she is perfectly free to abandon her trade and go into a shop or factory or into domestic service whenever the impulse strikes her; all the prevailing gabble about white slave jails and kidnappers comes from pious rogues who make a living by feeding such nonsense to the credulous. So long as the average prostitute is able to make a good living, she is quite content with her lot, and disposed to contrast it egotistically with the slavery of her virtuous sisters. If she complains of it, then you may be sure that her success is below her expectations. A starving lawyer always sees injustice in the courts. A bad physician is a bitter critic of Ehrlich and Pasteur. And when a suburban clergyman is forced out of his cure by a vestry-room revolution he almost invariably concludes that the sinfulness of man is incurable, and sometimes he even begins to doubt some of the typographical errors in Holy Writ.

The high value set upon virginity by men, whose esteem of it is based upon a mixture of vanity and voluptuousness, causes many women to guard it in

their own persons with a jealousy far beyond their
private inclinations and interests. It is their theory
that the loss of it would materially impair their
chances of marriage. This theory is not supported by
the facts. The truth is that the woman who sacrifices
her chastity, everything else being equal, stands a
much better chance of making a creditable marriage
than the woman who remains chaste. This is especially true of women of the lower economic classes.
At once they come into contact, hitherto socially difficult and sometimes almost impossible, with men of
higher classes, and begin to take on, with the curious
facility of their sex, the refinements and tastes and
points of view of those classes. The mistress thus
gathers charm, and what has begun as a sordid sale
of amiability not uncommonly ends with formal marriage. The number of such marriages is enormously
greater than appears superficially, for both parties
obviously make every effort to conceal the facts. Within
the circle of my necessarily limited personal acquaintance I know of scores of men, some of them of wealth
and position, who have made such marriages, and
who do not seem to regret it. It is an old observation,
indeed, that a woman who has previously disposed of
her virtue makes a good wife. The common theory
is that this is because she is grateful to her husband
for rescuing her from social outlawry; the truth is
that she makes a good wife because she is a shrewd
woman, and has specialized professionally in masculine
weakness, and is thus extra-competent at the traditional business of her sex. Such a woman often shows

a truly magnificent sagacity. It is very difficult to deceive her logically, and it is impossible to disarm her emotionally. Her revolt against the pruderies and sentimentalities of the world was evidence, to begin with, of her intellectual enterprise and courage, and her success as a rebel is proof of her extraordinary pertinacity, resourcefulness and acumen.

Even the most lowly prostitute is better off, in all worldly ways, than the virtuous woman of her own station in life. She has less work to do, it is less monotonous and dispiriting, she meets a far greater variety of men, and they are of classes distinctly beyond her own. Nor is her occupation hazardous and her ultimate fate tragic. A dozen or more years ago I observed a somewhat amusing proof of this last. At that time certain sentimental busybodies of the American city in which I lived undertook an elaborate inquiry into prostitution therein, and some of them came to me in advance, as a practical journalist, for advice as to how to proceed. I found that all of them shared the common superstition that the professional life of the average prostitute is only five years long, and that she invariably ends in the gutter. They were enormously amazed when they unearthed the truth. This truth was to the effect that the average prostitute of that town ended her career, not in the morgue but at the altar of God, and that those who remained unmarried often continued in practice for ten, fifteen and even twenty years, and then retired on competences. It was established, indeed, that fully eighty per cent. married, and that they almost always got husbands

who would have been far beyond their reach had they
remained virtuous. For one who married a cabman
or petty pugilist there were a dozen who married respectable mechanics, policemen, small shopkeepers and
minor officials, and at least two or three who married
well-to-do tradesmen and professional men. Among
the thousands whose careers were studied there was
actually one who ended as the wife of the town's
richest banker—that is, one who bagged the best catch
in the whole community. This woman had begun as
a domestic servant, and abandoned that harsh and
dreary life to enter a brothel. Her experiences there
polished and civilized her, and in her old age she
was a *grande dame* of great dignity. Much of the
sympathy wasted upon women of the ancient profession is grounded upon an error as to their own
attitude toward it. An educated woman, hearing that
a frail sister in a public stew is expected to be amiable
to all sorts of bounders, thinks of how *she* would
shrink from such contacts, and so concludes that the
actual prostitute suffers acutely. What she overlooks
is that these men, however gross and repulsive they
may appear to her, are measurably superior to men of
the prostitute's own class—say her father and brothers
—and that communion with them, far from being disgusting, is often rather romantic. I well remember
observing, during my collaboration with the vice-
crusaders aforesaid, the delight of a lady of joy who
had attracted the notice of a police lieutenant; she was
intensely pleased by the idea of having a client of
such haughty manners, such brilliant dress, and what

seemed to her to be so dignified a profession. It is
always forgotten that this weakness is not confined to
prostitutes, but runs through the whole female sex.
The woman who could not imagine an illicit affair
with a wealthy soap manufacturer or even with a
lawyer finds it quite easy to imagine herself succumb-
ing to an ambassador or a duke. There are very few
exceptions to this rule. In the most reserved of modern
societies the women who represent their highest flower
are notoriously complaisant to royalty. And royal wom-
en, to complete the circuit, not infrequently yield to
actors and musicians, *i.e.,* to men radiating a glamour
not encountered even in princes.

44. *The Future of Marriage*

HE TRANSVALUATION of val-
ues that is now in progress will go on slowly and for a
very long while. That it will ever be quite complete
is, of course, impossible. There are inherent differences that will continue to show themselves until the
end of time. As woman gradually becomes convinced,
not only of the possibility of economic independence,
but also of its value, she will probably lose her present
overmastering desire for marriage, and address herself to meeting men in free economic competition.

That is to say, she will address herself to acquiring that practical competence, that high talent for puerile and chiefly mechanical expertness, which now sets man ahead of her in the labour market of the world. To do this she will have to sacrifice some of her present intelligence; it is impossible to imagine a genuinely intelligent human being becoming a competent trial lawyer, or buttonhole worker, or newspaper sub-editor, or piano tuner, or house painter. Women, to get upon all fours with men in such stupid occupations, will have to commit spiritual suicide, which is probably much further than they will ever actually go. Thus a shade of their present superiority to men will always remain, and with it a shade of their relative inefficiency, and so marriage will remain attractive to them, or at all events to most of them, and its overthrow will be prevented. To abolish it entirely, as certain fevered reformers propose, would be as difficult as to abolish the precession of the equinoxes.

At the present time women vacillate somewhat absurdly between two schemes of life, the old and the new. On the one hand, their economic independence is still full of conditions, and on the other hand they are in revolt against the immemorial conventions. The result is a general unrest, with many symptoms of extravagant and unintelligent revolt. One of those symptoms is the appearance of intellectual striving in women—not a striving, alas, toward the genuine pearls and rubies of the mind, but one merely toward the acquirement of the rubber stamps that men employ in their so-called thinking. Thus we have women

who launch themselves into party politics, and fill
their heads with a vast mass of useless knowledge about
political tricks, customs, theories and personalities.
Thus, too, we have the woman social reformer, trailing
along ridiculously behind a tatterdemalion posse of
male utopians, each with something to sell. And thus
we have the woman who goes in for advanced wisdom of the sort on draught in women's clubs—in
brief, the sort of wisdom which consists entirely of a
body of beliefs and propositions that are ignorant,
unimportant and untrue. Such banal striving is most
prodigally on display in the United States, where
superficiality amounts to a national disease. Its popu-
larity is due to the relatively greater leisure of the
American people, who work less than any other people in the world, and, above all, to the relatively
greater leisure of American women. Thousands of
them have been emancipated from any compulsion
to productive labour without having acquired any
compensatory intellectual or artistic interest or social
duty. The result is that they swarm in the women's
clubs, and waste their time listening to bad poetry,
worse music, and still worse lectures on Maeterlinck,
Balkan politics and the subconscious. It is among such
women that one observes the periodic rages for
Bergsonism, the Montessori method, the twilight sleep
and other such follies, so pathetically characteristic of
American culture.

One of the evil effects of this tendency I have
hitherto descanted upon, to wit, the growing disposi-
tion of American women to regard all routine labour,

particularly in the home, as *infra dignitatem* and hence intolerable. Out of that notion arise many lamentable phenomena. On the one hand, we have the spectacle of a great number of healthy and well-fed women engaged in public activities that, nine times out of ten, are meaningless, mischievous and a nuisance, and on the other hand we behold such a decay in the domestic arts that, at the first onslaught of the late war, the national government had to import a foreign expert to teach the housewives of the country the veriest elements of thrift. No such instruction was needed by the housewives of the Continent. They were simply told how much food they could have, and their natural competence did the rest. There is never any avoidable waste there, either in peace or in war. A French housewife has little use for a garbage can, save as a depository for uplifting literature. She does her best with the means at her disposal, not only in war time but at all times.

As I have said over and over again in this inquiry, a woman's disinclination to acquire the intricate expertness that lies at the bottom of good housekeeping is due primarily to her active intelligence; it is difficult for her to concentrate her mind upon such stupid and meticulous enterprises. But whether difficult or easy, it is obviously important for the average woman to make some effort in that direction, for if she fails to do so there is chaos. That chaos is duly visible in the United States. Here women reveal one of their subterranean qualities: their deficiency in conscientiousness. They are quite without that dog-like fidelity to duty which is one of the shining marks of men. They never summon up a high pride in doing what is inherently disagreeable; they always go to the galleys under protest, and with vows of sabotage; their fundamental philosophy is almost that of the syndicalists. The sentimentality of men connives at this, and is thus largely responsible for it. Before the average *puella,* apprenticed in the kitchen, can pick up a fourth of the culinary subtleties that are common-place even to the chefs on dining cars, she has caught a man and need concern herself about them no more, for he has to eat, in the last analysis, whatever she sets before him, and his lack of intelligence makes it easy for her to shut off his academic criticisms by bald appeals to his emotions. By an easy process he finally attaches a positive value to her indolence. It is a proof, he concludes, of her fineness of soul. In the presence of her lofty incompetence he is abashed.

But as women, gaining economic autonomy, meet men in progressively bitterer competition, the rising masculine distrust and fear of them will be reflected even in the enchanted domain of marriage, and the husband, having yielded up most of his old rights, will begin to reveal a new jealousy of those that remain, and particularly of the right to a fair *quid pro quo* for his own docile industry. In brief, as women shake off their ancient disabilities they will also shake off some of their ancient immunities, and their doings will come to be regarded with a soberer and more exigent scrutiny than now prevails. The extension of the suffrage, I believe, will encourage this awakening; in wresting it from the reluctant male the women of the western world have planted dragons' teeth, the which will presently leap up and gnaw them. Now that women have the political power to obtain their just rights, they will begin to lose their old power to obtain special privileges by sentimental appeals. Men, facing them squarely, will consider them anew, not as romantic political and social invalids, to be coddled and caressed, but as free competitors in a harsh world. When that reconsideration gets under way there will be a general overhauling of the relations between the sexes, and some of the fair ones, I suspect, will begin to wonder why they didn't let well enough alone.

45. Effects of the War

THE PRESENT series of wars, it seems likely, will continue for twenty or thirty years, and perhaps longer. That the first clash was inconclusive was shown brilliantly by the preposterous nature of the peace finally reached—a peace so artificial and dishonest that the signing of it was almost equivalent to a new declaration of war. At least three new contests in the grand manner are plainly in sight— one between Germany and France to rectify the unnatural tyranny of a weak and incompetent nation over a strong and enterprising nation, one between Japan and the United States for the mastery of the Pacific, and one between England and the United States for the control of the sea. To these must be added various minor struggles, and perhaps one or two of almost major character: the effort of Russia to regain her old unity and power, the effort of the Turks to put down the slave rebellion (of Greeks, Armenians, Arabs, etc.) which now menaces them, the effort of the Latin Americans to throw off the galling Yankee yoke, and the joint effort of Russia and Germany (perhaps with England and Italy aiding) to get rid of such international nuisances as the insane Polish republic, the petty states of the Baltic, and perhaps also most of the Balkan states. I pass over the probability of a new mutiny in India, of the rising of China against the Japanese, and of a general struggle for a new alignment of boundaries in South America. All of these wars, great and small, are probable; most of them are humanly certain. They will be fought ferociously, and with the aid of destructive engines of the utmost efficiency. They will bring about an unparalleled butchery of men, and a large proportion of these men will be under forty years of age.

As a result there will be a shortage of husbands in Christendom, and as a second result the survivors will be appreciably harder to snare than the men of today. Every man of agreeable exterior and easy means will be pursued, not merely by a few dozen or score of women, as now, but by whole battalions and brigades of them, and he will be driven in sheer self-defence

into very sharp bargaining. Perhaps in the end the
state will have to interfere in the business, to prevent
the potential husband going to waste in the turmoil
of opportunity.

Just what form this interference is likely to take has
not yet appeared clearly. In France there is already
a wholesale legitimization of children born out of
wedlock and in Eastern Europe there has been a
clamour for the legalization of polygamy, but these
devices do not meet the main problem, which is the
encouragement of monogamy to the utmost. A plan
that suggests itself is the amelioration of the position
of the monogamous husband, now rendered increas-
ingly uncomfortable by the laws of most Christian
states. I do not think that the more intelligent sort of
women, faced by a perilous shortage of men, would
object seriously to that amelioration. They must see
plainly that the present system, if it is carried much
further, will begin to work powerfully against their
best interests, if only by greatly reinforcing the disinclination to marriage that already exists among the
better sort of men. The woman of true discretion, I
am convinced, would much rather marry a superior
man, even on unfavourable terms, than make John
Smith her husband, serf and prisoner at one stroke.

The law must eventually recognize this fact and
make provision for it. The average husband, perhaps,
deserves little succour. The woman who pursues and
marries him, though she may be moved by selfish aims,
should be properly rewarded by the state for her
service to it—a service surely not to be lightly estimated

in a military age. And that reward may conveniently take the form, as in the United States, of statutes giving her title to a large share of his real property and requiring him to surrender most of his income to her, and releasing her from all obedience to him and from all obligation to keep his house in order. But the woman who aspires to higher game should be quite willing, it seems to me, to resign some of these advantages in compensation for the greater honour and satisfaction of being wife to a man of merit, and mother to his children. All that is needed is laws allowing her, if she will, to resign her right of dower, her right to maintenance and her immunity from discipline, and to make any other terms that she may be led to regard as equitable. At present women are unable to make most of these concessions even if they would: the laws of the majority of western nations are inflexible. If, for example, an Englishwoman should agree, by an ante-nuptial contract, to submit herself to the discipline, not of the current statutes, but of the elder common law, which allowed a husband to correct his wife corporally with a stick no thicker than his thumb, it would be competent for any sentimental neighbour to set the agreement at naught by haling her husband before a magistrate for carrying it out, and it is a safe wager that the magistrate would jail him.

This plan, however novel it may seem, is actually already in operation. Many a married woman, in order to keep her husband from revolt, makes more or less disguised surrenders of certain of the rights and immunities that she has under existing laws. There are, for example, even in America, women who practise the domestic arts with competence and diligence, despite the plain fact that no legal penalty would be visited upon them if they failed to do so. There are women who follow external trades and professions, contributing a share to the family exchequer. There are women who obey their husbands, even against their best judgments. There are, most numerous of all, women who wink discreetly at husbandly departures, overt or in mere intent, from the oath of chemical purity taken at the altar. It is a commonplace, indeed, that many happy marriages admit a party of the third part. There would be more of them if there were more women with enough serenity of mind to see the practical advantage of the arrangement. The trouble with such triangulations is not primarily that they involve perjury or that they offer any fundamental offence to the wife; if she avoids banal theatricals, in fact, they commonly have the effect of augmenting the husband's devotion to her and respect for her, if only as the fruit of comparison. The trouble with them is that very few men among us have sense enough to manage them intelligently. The masculine mind is readily taken in by specious values; the average married man of Protestant Christendom, if he succumbs at all, succumbs to some meretricious and flamboyant creature, bent only upon fleecing him. Here is where the harsh realism of the Frenchman shows its superiority to the sentimentality of the men of the Teutonic races. A Frenchman would no more

think of taking a mistress without consulting his wife
than he would think of standing for office without
consulting his wife. The result is that he is seldom
victimized. For one Frenchman ruined by women
there are at least a hundred Englishmen and Americans, despite the fact that a hundred times as many
Frenchmen engage in that sort of recreation. The case
of Zola is typical. As is well known, his amours were
carefully supervised by Mme. Zola from the first
days of their marriage, and in consequence his life
was wholly free from scandals and his mind was never
distracted from his work.

46. The Eternal Romance

BUT WHATEVER the future
of monogamous marriage, there will never be any
decay of that agreeable adventurousness which now
lies at the bottom of all transactions between the
sexes. Women may emancipate themselves, they may
borrow the whole bag of masculine tricks, and they
may cure themselves of their present desire for the
vegetable security of marriage, but they will never
cease to be women, and so long as they are women
they will remain provocative to men. Their chief
charm today lies precisely in the fact that they are

dangerous, that they threaten masculine liberty and autonomy, that their sharp minds present a menace vastly greater than that of acts of God and the public enemy—and they will be dangerous for ever. Men fear them, and are fascinated by them. They know how to show their teeth charmingly; the more enlightened of them have perfected a superb technique of fascination. It was Nietzsche who called them the recreation of the warrior—not of the poltroon, remember, but of the warrior. A profound saying. They have an infinite capacity for rewarding masculine industry and enterprise with small and irresistible flatteries; their acute understanding combines with their capacity for evoking ideas of beauty to make them incomparable companions when the serious business of the day is done, and the time has come to expand comfortably in the interstellar ether.

Every man, I daresay, has his own notion of what constitutes perfect peace and contentment, but all of those notions, despite the fundamental conflict of the sexes, revolve around women. As for me—and I hope I may be pardoned, at this late stage in my inquiry, for intruding my own personality—I reject the two commonest of them: passion, at least in its more adventurous and melodramatic aspects, is too exciting and alarming for so indolent a man, and I am too egoistic to have much desire to be mothered. What, then, remains for me? Let me try to describe it to you.

It is the close of a busy and vexatious day—say half past five or six o'clock of a winter afternoon. I have had a cocktail or two, and am stretched out on a

divan in front of a fire, smoking. At the edge of the
divan, close enough for me to reach her with my
hand, sits a woman not too young, but still good-
looking and well-dressed—above all, a woman with a
soft, low-pitched, agreeable voice. As I snooze she
talks—of anything, everything, all the things that
women talk of: books, music, the play, men, other
women. No politics. No business. No religion. No
metaphysics. Nothing challenging and vexatious—but
remember, she is intelligent; what she says is clearly
expressed, and often picturesquely. I observe the fine
sheen of her hair, the pretty cut of her frock, the glint
of her white teeth, the arch of her eye-brow, the
graceful curve of her arm. I listen to the exquisite
murmur of her voice. Gradually I fall asleep—but only
for an instant. At once, observing it, she raises her
voice ever so little, and I am awake. Then to sleep
again—slowly and charmingly down that slippery hill
of dreams. And then awake again, and then asleep
again, and so on.

I ask you seriously: could anything be more unutterably beautiful? The sensation of falling asleep
is to me the most exquisite in the world. I delight in
it so much that I even look forward to death itself
with a sneaking wonder and desire. Well, here is sleep
poetized and made doubly sweet. Here is sleep set to
the finest music in the world. I match this situation
against any that you can think of. It is not only enchanting; it is also, in a very true sense, ennobling.
In the end, when the girl grows prettily miffed and
throws me out, I return to my sorrows somehow

purged and glorified. I am a better man in my own sight. I have grazed upon the fields of asphodel. I have been genuinely, completely and unregrettably happy.

47. *Apologia in Conclusion*

T THE END I crave the indulgence of the cultured reader for the imperfections necessarily visible in all that I have here set down —imperfections not only due to incomplete information and fallible logic, but also, and perhaps more importantly, to certain fundamental weaknesses of the sex to which I have the honour to belong. A man is inseparable from his congenital vanities and stupidities, as a dog is inseparable from its fleas. They reveal themselves in everything he says and does, but they reveal themselves most of all when he discusses the majestic mystery of woman. Just as he smirks and rolls his eyes in her actual presence, so he puts on a pathetic and unescapable clownishness when he essays to dissect her in the privacy of the laboratory. There is no book on woman by a man that is not a stupendous compendium of posturings and imbecilities. There are but two books that show even a superficial desire to be honest—"The Unexpurgated Case Against Woman

Suffrage," by Sir Almroth Wright, and this one. Wright made a gallant attempt to tell the truth, but before he got half way through his task his ineradicable donkeyishness as a male overcame his scientific frenzy as a psychologist, and so he hastily washed his hands of the business, and affronted the judicious with a half-baked and preposterous book. Perhaps I have failed too, and even more ingloriously. If so, I am full of sincere and indescribable regret.

THE END

Library of Congress Cataloguing in Publication Data

Mencken, H. L. (Henry Louis), 1880-1956.
In defense of women.
(Time reading program special edition)
Reprint. Originally published: New York: Time, [1963]
Issued in case, with: Attending marvels/George Gaylord Simpson.
1. Women—Social conditions.
I. Title. II. Series.
[HQ1221.M5 1982]   305.4   82-846 AACR2
ISBN 0-8094-3722-8
ISBN 0-8094-3723-6 (pbk.)